Hold Infinity in the palm of your hand

And Eternity in an hour

ETERNITY REVISITED

Also by Stuart Harris:

The Severed Hand, a medieval drama broadcast by BBC Radio Sheffield [1979]

Themes and Images: Singaporean and Malaysian Poetry in English [1989]

The Human Factor: a critical guide to the novel by Graham Greene [1990]

Cosmologia: A Sequence of Epic Poems by Erasmus Darwin (ed.) [2002]

Erasmus Darwin's Enlightenment Epic: A Critical Study [2002]

The Prince, My Son, Our Hero: Three Elegies by Erasmus Darwin (ed.) [2009]

Poems of Lichfield and Derby by Erasmus Darwin (ed.) [2011]

Poems of School and University by Erasmus Darwin (ed.) [2012]

Erratum: *John Hall's* should read *John Wallis's.*

The cover design, drawn by the author, is of an hour-glass crossed by John Hall's symbol for infinity/eternity. The circumferences of the two shapes describe four serpentine lines, William Hogarth's 'line of beauty'.

ETERNITY REVISITED

A Meditation

on

Time and the Timeless

Stuart Harris

Dedicated with love and gratitude to my family

First Edition: Published in 2021 by Stuart Harris

171 Millhouses Lane, Sheffield, S7 2HD

Printed by Print2Demand, Westoning

ISBN 978-0-95-421517-0

***In Memoriam*: Thomas M. Kershaw, MA**

Who inspired me as my literature teacher at Chesterfield Grammar School, 1955-58

From: *Ode: Intimations of Immortality from Recollections of Early Childhood*

Our birth is but a sleep and a forgetting:
The soul that rises with us, our life's Star,
Hath had elsewhere its setting,
And cometh from afar:
Not in entire forgetfulness,
And not in utter nakedness,
But trailing clouds of glory do we come
From God, who is our home:
Heaven lies about us in our infancy!
Shades of the prison-house begin to close
Upon the growing Boy,
But he beholds the light, and whence it flows,
He sees it in his joy;
The Youth, who daily farther from the east
Must travel, still is Nature's Priest,
And by the vision splendid
Is on his way attended;
At length the Man perceives it die away,
And fade into the light of common day. [Lines 58-76]

*****

The clouds that gather round the setting sun
Do take a sobering colour from an eye
That hath kept watch o'er man's mortality;
Another race hath been, and other palms are won.
Thanks to the human heart by which we live,
Thanks to its tenderness, its joys, and fears,
To me the meanest flower that blows can give
Thoughts that do often lie too deep for tears. [Lines 200-207]

William Wordsworth (1770-1850)

CONTENTS

EPIGRAPH

In your sight, Lord, the whole world is like a grain of
dust that tips the scales,
like a drop of morning dew falling on the ground.
Yet you are merciful to all,
because you can do all things and overlook men's sins
so that they can repent.
Yes, you love all that exists, you hold nothing of what
you have made in abhorrence,
for had you hated anything, you would not have
formed it.
And how, had you not willed it, could a thing persist,
how be conserved if not called forth by you?
You spare all things because all things are yours,
Lord, lover of life,
you whose imperishable spirit is in all.

The *Holy Bible*: Book of Wisdom, chapter 11.
(N.B. Found in Catholic editions; otherwise Apocryphal)

Author's Note

In the same week of June 2013 that my wife Marie died from cancer, a meteorite shower was announced by astronomers. We had always looked up to the sky together at such times. At around 10pm I parked in an area of high moorland near our home and looked up at the sky. At that moment Marie's absence struck me. "Where are you?" I shouted instinctively. Then I saw a hawk hovering over the heather. I heard another bird's alarm call and I saw a curlew with her chick hurrying through the undergrowth.

I did not see the hawk take the chick but the chick was gone and I heard the bereft curlew's cries. The meteorites and their fiery meeting with the atmosphere were forgotten after the earthly event I had just witnessed. I drove back in my grief to my empty nest.

This essay is in part a reply to the question I had shouted into the night.

*****

N.B. Quotations from the *Holy Bible* are taken from the Catholic Douay Version, 1609, revised edition, 1956.

*****

Eternity Revisited

Part One: On Space and Time

Approximately 13.8* billion (13,800,000,000) years ago - the time currently calculated to have elapsed since the 'Big Bang' - the universe as we know it began, or came into being. This beginning was an incalculably dense point, a 'singularity', which 'exploded', scattering or 'inflating' its physical components in all directions simultaneously and almost evenly. This event was the beginning of the space-time continuum in which all material entities exist. Logically, 'before' this event is a concept that has no meaning.

However, there is a concept that maybe offers some insight into this scenario: Eternity, together with its corollary, Infinity. In order to understand 'eternity' correctly in this context, we have to discard any ideas of endless time and of boundless space that commonly attach themselves to these concepts. The Romantic poet William Blake's vision: "Hold infinity in the palm of your hand/And eternity in an hour" remains physical and time-bound as imagery. In contrast, his statement "Eternity is in love with the productions of Time" is a wonderfully expressed truth. The eternal loving creator has a permanent relationship with the created temporal universe: a bond of love. It is storge+, the love of parents for their child; and perhaps of a scientist or artist for their work.

As parents will protect and correct their child, and a scientist or artist will attempt to perfect their work, so the Creator did, and will, fine tune the cosmos in the interests of the evolution of life, "the productions of Time".

From the moment of the 'Big Bang' - actually a silent moment - time can be measured in our cosmos: 13.8 billion years have elapsed since that first moment. It was a moment that 'budded off' Eternity into temporal existence, while still, like a child, in a developmental relationship with its parent.

* This figure is based on observations by the [Max] Planck Space Observatory between 2009 and 2013 of the cosmic microwave background, and subsequent calculations.

\+ The Greek word *Storge* (pronounced Stor-gi or Stor-ji) adopted into English means 'parental love'. I prefer the hard 'g'.

On Space and Time

Already at the moment of the 'Big Bang' the physical laws governing the cosmos's rapid inflation were fully active. Eternity/Infinity expressed itself in the singularity that was programmed to initiate the finite, material universe. In our current reckoning, the singularity was concentrated into the smallest space, the densest volume, we can imagine.

The Infinite does not hold the same perspective that we do. The question of what existed before the 'Big Bang' is unanswerable except in terms of a creative act initiated in the Eternal and Infinite mode of being. Space did not exist before Time began and *vice versa*. Eternity, a mode of being without the dimension of Time, combined with Infinity, a mode of existence without the dimensions of space, produced the cosmologist's 'singularity' from which the space-time continuum we know as the universe grew.

The space and time inaugurated at the 'Big Bang' had the patterns and laws of their evolution 'imprinted' in them, as well as the patterns and laws of their dissolution. Albert Einstein's formula $E=MC^2$ provides the parameters: Energy = Mass x The Speed of Light Squared. Once again, William Blake expresses the relationship between Eternity-Infinity and the cosmos with great insight: "Energy is eternal delight".

A thought here, derived from Quantum Theory, is that because the material and energetic universe is 'connected', through its origin to the immaterial eternal-infinite mode of being, especially at the subatomic level, it may slip in and out of existence. Furthermore, apocalyptic scenarios such as the cosmologist's 'heat death' of the universe may anticipate or dramatize the return of our temporal-spatial cosmos to the eternal-infinite mode.

The above are the kind of issues that arise when time and eternity, the measurable universe and infinity, are juxtaposed. Matters can also be confused when the cosmos is described as 'finite but unbounded'; i.e. an expanding universe spontaneously creating space and time as it expands. The question of what existed before the 'Big Bang' remains an issue in this scenario. Also, what exists beyond the frontier of such an expansion is another perfectly legitimate question in considering the physical parameters of the universe.

On Space and Time

Suffice it to say here that the 'Steady State' theory of the universe, which would have accommodated notions of a materially eternal cosmos, has been rejected by cosmologists who have identified and measured the cosmic background radiation left behind by the 'Big Bang'. These measurements prove that the universe did indeed have a beginning 13.8 billion years ago. Since that moment of time, which was also the beginning of Time itself, the cosmos — the galaxies of stars, the star systems including our own solar system, the planets including our own Earth — have been evolving according to certain laws. On Earth life began 4,280,000,000 years ago with a continuing history of changes, developments and extinctions into the present time. But the Earth, it must be remembered, is a very, very tiny object within an already vast cosmos with its billions of stars - as many stars as there are grains of sand on all the Earth's beaches, it has been said. To see the Earth in this context is to perplex the mind; only tempered perhaps by the fact that we humans seem to be positioned, in terms of size, in the middle of the scale of material things - the smallest atomic particles are in a similar ratio to us as we are to the stars of the galaxies. Alexander Pope's assessment of humanity's position in the scheme of things is apposite here: "Placed on this isthmus of a middle state" [*Essay on Man, 1733-4*]

In terms of time, the Sun on which we are so dependent is middle-aged, being about 4.6 billion years old, and its eventual demise by cooling and expanding into a Red Giant that will swallow the Earth is reckoned to be another five billion years into the future. Meanwhile the universe may keep expanding and cooling into an unknown future: a 'heat death', a 'big crunch', a 'big rip', a metamorphosis into another kind of universe, and other speculative scenarios promoted by cosmologists. The numbers, the 'powers' in mathematical terms governing these various scenarios, are scarcely meaningful to us except through their mathematical expression. Within this extended time-frame, the history of hominin life on Earth is brief: two and a half million years, and less than that for *Homo sapiens.* The time-line of the geological record extends six hundred and fifty million years into the past with the first traces of life. During this extended time there have been major extinctions of life-forms: for example, at the end of the Permian Period two hundred and fifty million years ago, and the extinction of the Dinosaurs at the end of the Cretaceous Period, fifty million years ago.

On Space and Time

We have learned of these extinction events through our study of the fossil record, because, of course, no human eyes existed to see the drama of life on Earth unfolding in Time. Quite simply there was no human audience watching the various acts of the play. Nevertheless, we have notes on the script provided by the fossil record and various scientific measurements - of radioactive decay, for example.

So we have to accept that for most of Earth's history there was no self-conscious intelligence such as we possess in existence on the entire Earth. I do not wish to discount the intelligence shown by other creatures on land, in the sea and in the air. But *Homo sapiens*, or Modern Man, most probably has a unique ability to remember and record past time, not only of ourselves as individuals but as a community in time and space.

As a species, we have now reached a point in our evolution when we can measure and manipulate the material Earth on most scales of existence. We have also made a start on observing and measuring the cosmos itself, and we are engaged in the discovery of the basic laws of matter, governing the behaviour of everything on the very smallest and the very largest scales. We are intent on achieving, as Stephen Hawking says in the 'Conclusion' to his *A Brief History of Time* [1988], "the ultimate triumph of human reason - for then we would know the mind of God".

This is in part a final rhetorical flourish, but he believes that we would understand the physical laws, expressed in mathematical equations, that made possible and that underpin the material cosmos. A 'unified theory' or 'theory of everything' would validate Albert Einstein's firmly held belief that "God does not play dice" with the universe.

However, the scientific pursuit of physical laws, with the assumption derived from Ancient Greek Ionian philosophy that everything has a rational explanation, excludes much of human experience as expressed in literature. The *Holy Bible*, for example, tells us much about the 'mind of God' which is not susceptible to rational explanation. The life of Jesus Christ contains many events which run counter to our understanding of physical laws. So much so that we have to accept that our 'ordinary' world is susceptible to extra-ordinary interventions. I shall return to the implications of this statement later.

On Space and Time

At this point I should like to state a proposition: that the temporal cosmos is temporary and that there is another 'mode of being' which is non-temporal, i.e. eternal. The 'Big Bang ' theory of the origin of the cosmos as we know it makes such a conclusion difficult to avoid. Admittedly, some cosmologists seek to avoid it by positing a 'multiverse': a multitude of other universes in company with our own but which are built according to parameters not measurable by us. Or again, that our cosmos might metamorphose itself into a new cosmos at the end-point of our own.

It must be said that we have no scientific evidence for either of these alternative scenarios at the present time. They are based on what cosmologists call 'thought experiments'.

Conversely, our current scientific data supports the view that our cosmos had a beginning, that it is evolving through time, and that, with our current understanding of physical laws, it will have an ending. We may also assert, with St Augustine of Hippo, that time is a property only of the universe that God created, not a dimension in which God is normally to be found. I would also add, however, that God **can** act in the temporal and physical dimensions - a fact for which we have ample evidence in the Bible and in the histories of Jesus Christ, of the Saints and of believers generally.

To repeat William Blake's statement: "Eternity is in love with the productions of Time". This loving relationship between God and His creation, His creatures, is the central message of Jesus Christ as witnessed in the *New Testament*. Indeed, the incarnation of Jesus Christ is the greatest act of love performed by God the Father for the benefit of His children.

In addition, both *Old* and *New Testaments* of the *Holy Bible* reveal a third Person or agency who has the power to act in the temporal and physical world: the Holy Spirit, sometimes referred to as Wisdom, or Paraclete. In St John's *Gospel* [chapter 14, vss. 16-17] we read:

> *And I will ask the Father; and He shall give you another Paraclete, that He might abide with you for ever; the Spirit of Truth, whom the world cannot receive, because it seeth Him not, nor knoweth Him. But you shall know Him; because He shall abide with you and shall be in you.*

This is the third person of the Trinity to some of whose actions I shall return later in this book. It is notable that Jesus Christ here refers to the Holy Spirit as "another Paraclete", thus indicating that He Himself, the second person of the Trinity, was also a "Paraclete", advocate or comforter. This title for Jesus Christ is given by John in his *First Epistle* [chapter two, vs. 1]: "we have an advocate with the Father, Jesus Christ the just". The Greek word *Paracletos* is used on both occasions.

*****

Complementary *Meditations* of Thomas Traherne

From *Centuries of Meditations*, 1673

H.M. Margoliouth, Traherne's editor, writes: *Thomas Traherne's Handbook to Felicity.* That was the purpose of the *Centuries.* Traherne in London wrote for Mrs Susanna Hopton in Herefordshire. He wanted to share with her the 'profitable wonders' he had discovered... Traherne gave the book no title. If he had, it would probably have been 'The Way to Felicity' or something of that sort. At a later date an unknown hand wrote 'Centuries of Meditations' on one of the unused pages at the beginning. Dobell [the printer] used that as its title when he first published the book in 1908. It was a natural thing to do, but a mistake because misleading. Though some of the sections, especially in the second half of the first Century, may properly be called meditation, the majority may not, and the intention of the book is not meditation but instruction.

*****

Importance of Meditation [Fourth Century, No. 96]

To be acquainted with celestial things is not only to know them, but by frequent meditation to be familiar with them. The effects of which are admirable. For by this, those things that at first seemed uncertain become evident, those things which seemed remote become near, those things which appeared like shady clouds become solid realities: finally, those things which seemed impertinent to us and of little concernment, appear to be our own, according to the strictest rules of propriety and of infinite moment.

*****

Human Understanding [First Century, No. 19]

Alas the WORLD is but a little centre in comparison of you [reader]. *Suppose it millions of miles from the Earth to the Heavens* [visible universe], *and millions of millions above the Stars, both here and over the heads of our Antipodes: it is surrounded with infinite and eternal space. And like a gentleman's house to one that is travelling; it is a long time before you come unto it, you pass it in an instant, and leave it for ever. The Omnipresence and Eternity of God are your fellows and companions. And all that is in them ought to be made your familiar Treasures. Your understanding comprehends the World like the dust of a balance, measures Heaven with a span, and esteems a thousand years but as one day. So that Great, Endless, Eternal Delights are only fit to be its enjoyments.*

*****

Complementary *Meditations* of Thomas Traherne

The Universe Designed for Humankind [Second Century, No. 89]

What would Heaven and Earth be worth, were there no spectator, no enjoyer? As much therefore as the end is better than the means, the thought of the World whereby it is enjoyed is better than the World. So is the idea of it in the Soul of Man, better than the World in the esteem of God: it being the end [final purpose] *of the World, without which Heaven and Earth would be in vain. It is better to you, because by it you receive the World, and it is the tribute you pay. It more immediately beautifies and perfects your nature. How deformed you would be should all the World stand about you and you be idle? Were you able to create other worlds, God would rather you should think on this. For thereby you are united to Him. The sun in your eye is as much to you as the sun in the Heavens. For by this the other is enjoyed. It would shine on all rivers, trees, and beasts in vain to you could you not think upon it. The sun in your understanding illuminates your Soul, the sun in the heavens enlightens the hemisphere. The world within you is an offering returned, which is infinitely more acceptable to God Almighty, since it came from Him, that it might return unto Him. Wherein the mystery is great. For God hath made you able to create worlds in your own mind which are more precious unto Him than those which He created; and to give and offer up the world unto Him, which is very delightful in flowing from Him, but much more in returning to Him.*

*****

God's Invisibility [Second Century, No. 19]

They that quarrel at the manner of God's revealing Himself are troubled because He is invisible. Yet it is expedient that He should be so: for whatsoever is visible is a body; whatsoever is a body excludeth other things out of the place where itself is. If God therefore being infinite were visible He would make it impossible for anything to have a being. Besides, bulk as such in itself is dead. Whatsoever is visible is so in like manner. That which inspireth bulk with motion, life, and sense with a bodily presence, is invisible; and in itself distinct from the bulk which it inspireth. Were God therefore pure bulk, He would neither move nor will, nor desire anything; but being invisible, He leaveth room for and effecteth all things. He filleth nothing with a bodily presence, but includeth all. He is pure Life, Knowledge and Desire, from which all things flow: pure Wisdom, Goodness, and Love to which all things return

*****

Complementary *Meditations* of Thomas Traherne

The Creation Exists Eternally In God [Third Century, No. 65]

With this we are delighted because it is absolutely impossible that any Power dwelling with Love should continue idle. Since God therefore was infinitely and eternally communicative, all things were contained in Him from all Eternity. As Nazianzen in his 38th Oration admirably expresseth it in these words: "Because it was by no means sufficient for GOODNESS to move only in contemplation of itself: but it became what was GOOD to be diffused and propagated, that more might be affected with the benefit (for this was the part of the Highest GOODNESS): first He thought upon angelical and celestial virtues, and that thought was the work He wrought by the WORD and fulfilled by the SPIRIT.* ***Atque ita Secundi Splendores procreati Primi Splendoris Administria.*** *" (And so were there Second Splendours* [angels and archangels] *created and made to minister to the First Splendour* [God]*), so that all motions, successions, creatures, and operations with their beginnings and ends were in Him from Everlasting. To whom nothing can be added because from all Eternity He was whatsoever to all Eternity He can be. All things being now to be seen and contemplated in His bosom; and advanced therefore into a Divine Light, being infinitely older and more precious than we were aware.* ***Time itself being in God eternally*** [my emphasis].

*St Gregory of Nazianzus [329-389], Bishop of Constantinople. Doctor of the Greek Orthodox Church.

*****

We Were Made In God's Image [Third Century, No. 58]

In discovering the matter or objects to be enjoyed, I was greatly aided by remembering that we were made in God's Image. For thereupon it must of necessity follow that God's Treasures be our Treasures, and His joys our joys. So that by enquiring what were God's I found the objects of our Felicity, God's Treasures being ours. For we were made in His Image that we might live in His similitude. And herein I was mightily confirmed by the Apostle's blaming the Gentiles, and charging it upon them as a very great fault that they were alienated from the life of God, for hereby ***I perceived that we were to live the life of God when we lived the true life of nature according to knowledge*** [my emphasis]: *and that by blindness and corruption we had strayed from it. Now God's Treasures are His own perfections, and all His creatures.*

*****

Eternity Revisited

Part Two: On Time and the Timeless

One of the consequences of our physical existence is that we live in a world of ups and downs. This results in a mental habit of attaching spiritual (and even moral) values to movements and locations that involve up or down, high or low. A representative instance of this profound link between physical and spiritual behaviour might be taken from the Psalms:

> *I have lifted up my eyes to the mountains, from whence help shall come to me.*
>
> [Book of *Psalms*, number 20, vs. 1]

A picturesque example of this is Jacob's dream of a ladder reaching from Earth to Heaven:

> *And he saw in his sleep a ladder standing upon the earth, and the top thereof touching heaven; the angels also of God ascending and descending by it.*
>
> [Book of *Genesis*, chapter 28, vs. 12]

We have become used to convenient terms for spiritual events that bind us to the physical. A key example is to be found in the Apostles' Creed:

> *He* ***descended*** *into Hell; On the third day he* **rose** *again from the dead; He* ***ascended*** *into heaven.*

The **Assumption**, the taking up into Heaven of the Virgin Mary on her death, is another important example. Here God transfigured her mortal body, thus avoiding its corruption. In the medieval period these movement words were taken to have a literal meaning in a geocentric universe. So, Heaven was above the fixed stars, and Hell was at the burning centre of the Earth. Our current scientific cosmological model excludes such a belief, and therefore the movement up and down to heaven and hell has no literal meaning; it can only be taken metaphorically. What the movement represents is the moment of change from the temporal to the non-temporal mode of being. There are many places in the *New Testament* where this change occurs. The Transfiguration of Jesus Christ is perhaps the most revealing, since it was witnessed by three disciples: Peter, James and John, and it took place in space (the top of a mountain) and time (while praying):

On Time and the Timeless

> *And whilst he prayed the shape of his countenance was altered and his raiment became white and glittering. And, behold, two men were with him. And they were Moses and Elias* [Elijah].
>
> [St Luke's *Gospel*, chapter nine, vss. 30-31]

St Matthew has a very similar account in his *Gospel*:

> *And he was transfigured before them. And his face did shine as the Sun; and his garments became white as snow.* [chapter seventeen, vs. 2]

There are many other occasions in the *New Testament* which throw light on this change in mode of being and which I shall come to later.

Sufficient to say at this point that the presence of Moses and Elijah in the Disciples' reported account tells us that Eternity has materialized in Time on this occasion. However, I should like first to set out a 'general principle' for this kind of change or transformation.

It is well established by current cosmological findings that our universe had a beginning in a 'Big Bang'. I like to think of this event as the **conception** of the cosmos, both in the sense of the beginning of a physical development and in the sense of the idea of the cosmos becoming a reality.

This second meaning is contained within the opening statement of St John's *Gospel*:

> *In the beginning was the Word, and the Word was with God, and the Word was God. The same was in the beginning with God. All things were made by Him; and without Him was made nothing that was made.*

Thus in the Timeless Mode of being, God conceived of what we call the 'space-time continuum' and brought it into material existence. This act of God also established the relationship between God (the Timeless Being) and his creation of the cosmos in Time.

This relationship is therefore 'causal' in the literal sense of the word. So we are to understand that there is a channel open between the Timeless and Time. The Creation, the Big Bang, was not (as Deists would argue) the only occasion when God connected with, and acted on, the material universe.

On Time and the Timeless

Evolutionary biologists are now becoming aware that the development of life on Earth has only been possible if the behaviour of matter at all levels was 'tweaked' in ways that have preserved and sustained its existence. The structure of DNA, now considered too complicated to be the result of random mutations, is a major example. The 'argument from design' has returned as an argument supportable by scientific evidence, from the large cosmic scale to the small scale of atomic particles.

The Biblical narrative is, of course, predicated on acts of God in the history of the Jewish people and of subsequent Christianity.

This may be the place to consider the 'Personality' of God. In this I wish to avoid all the various controversies that historically have swirled around the doctrine of the Trinity. My idea of the Trinity is derived from my emphasis on the Timeless character of God. The full acceptance of this concept necessitates an understanding that the Trinity - Father, Son and Holy Spirit - have always existed outside of time. In other words, no one 'person' of the Trinity can possibly come into being after another of the three Persons.

Therefore it may be confusing to think too literally about the Father-Son relationship, especially since both are immortals, as is the Holy Spirit, which has historically been difficult to imagine as other than a dove or a flame. These icons deflect us from the knowledge that the Trinity is Three Persons in one God.

The Holy Spirit is a person. The *New Testament* images of the Holy Spirit, such as the Dove that descended on Jesus Christ at His baptism by St John, (in the *Gospels* of St Matthew, St Mark and St Luke); or the post-Pentecostal event in the *Acts of the Apostles*, chapter two, when the Holy Ghost as tongues of flame rested on the Apostles and gave them the gift of universal language. At other times the Holy Spirit is realized as breath.

These manifestations must be understood as signs and instruments of God the Holy Spirit, materializing as phenomena in the physical world. Unlike God the Father, who is never seen in Person by any human being, but whose voice may be heard, as here by Moses, from the 'burning bush':

> *God said to Moses: I AM WHO I AM. He said: Thus shalt thou say to the children of Israel: HE WHO IS hath sent me to you.*

[The Book of *Exodus*, chapter 3, vs.14]

On Time and the Timeless

It is clear from this example that God the Father is a Person who - and the syntax makes this very clear - is Timeless. The incarnation of Jesus Christ, of course, establishes His combined Divine and human nature.

The title 'Trinity', abstract as it is, deflects attention from the Person-hood of the Holy Spirit. The *Kyrie* in the liturgy of the Catholic Church addresses each of the Three Persons of the Trinity in these terms:

> *Kyrie Eleison* (Lord Have Mercy);
> *Christe Eleison* (Christ Have Mercy);
> *Kyrie Eleison* (Lord Have Mercy).

Liturgically the first '*Kyrie*' refers to God the Father; the second to Jesus Christ; and the third to the Holy Spirit as 'Lord'. As we have seen, the iconography of the Church does not usually reflect this fact of the Holy Spirit as a Person. The question of whether the Holy Spirit 'proceeded' from the Father only, or from the Father and the Son, fuelled the schism between the Greek Orthodox and the Roman Catholic Churches in the 11th century. I prefer to believe that the Holy Spirit 'proceeded' from neither, but, like Father and Son, is a distinct, if not separate, Person of the Trinity.

This might be the appropriate point to address the patriarchal character of our reading and thinking about God. The paternal status of God as Father is, of course, bound up with Jesus Christ as the only Son of God. This relationship would appear to identify Jesus Christ as a younger generation, begotten by the first generation, God the Father, in the eternal sphere.

Given the timeless nature of Eternity, we must accept that the Three Persons of the Trinity cannot be subject to generational relationships. Indeed, Jesus Christ Himself told His disciples, "Before Abraham was, I am" [St John's *Gospel*, chapter 8, vs.58], a statement that is unequivocal about His eternal, timeless nature. The opening verses of St John's *Gospel* confirm this:

> *In the beginning was the Word, and the Word was with God, and the Word was God. The same was in the beginning with God.*

On Time and the Timeless

The "Word" is *logos* in Greek and refers to Jesus Christ, whose prayer for His disciples, also in St John's *Gospel*, confirms Jesus Christ's eternal existence:

> *And now glorify thou me, O Father, with thyself, with the glory which I had* ***before the world was,*** [my emphasis] *with thee.* [chapter 17, vs. 5]

'Glory' refers to the light of Eternity and to the Eternal Mode in which Jesus Christ lived before he became human as the Only Son of God on Earth. It was at the Incarnation that Jesus Christ became 'the Son of God' in the material and temporal world. In order for Jesus Christ to be born to Mary at that particular moment in history (an event which some theologians have referred to as 'the scandal of particularity') there needed to be a creative impulse from the Holy Spirit in the Timeless Mode being effective in a precisely timed physical conception.

The coming pregnancy is offered to Mary by the Angel Gabriel: "The Holy Ghost shall come upon thee and the power of the Most High shall overshadow thee" [St Luke's *Gospel*, chapter 1, vs.35]. In St Matthew's *Gospel*, the account is more matter-of-fact:

> *When His mother Mary was espoused to Joseph, before they came together, she was found with child, of the Holy Ghost.* [chapter 1, vs.18]

In spite of tradition, it cannot strictly speaking be said that the reference in the Book of *Genesis* [chapter one, vs. 2] to the spirit of God that "moved over the waters" at the creation of the cosmos is the Holy Spirit. Judaism is a monotheistic religion: the Holy Spirit of the Trinity 'belongs' to Christianity. Yet the Holy Spirit is eternal and not definable by religious dogma.

God the Father is usually active as a voice and on at least one occasion, the baptism of Jesus Christ, in company with a 'materialization' of the Holy Spirit:

> *And Jesus, being baptized, forthwith came out of the water; and lo, the heavens were opened to Him, and He saw the Spirit of God descending as a dove and coming upon Him. And, behold, a voice from heaven saying: This is my be- loved Son, in whom I am well pleased.* [St. Matthew's *Gospel*, chapter 3, vss. 16-17]

Here the three Persons of the Trinity have 'materialized', entered Time at one and the same moment in history.

Yet, in spite of this Divine declaration of sonship, Jesus Christ never refers to Himself, nor uses the title, 'the Son of God', but rather 'the Son of Man'. I should perhaps qualify this by saying that Jesus Christ, in the *Gospels*, does indeed claim to be the Son of God:

> *All things are delivered to me by my Father, and no-one knoweth the Son but the Father, nor does anyone know the Father save the Son and he to whom it shall please the Son to reveal Him.* [St Matthew, chapter 11, vs. 27. See also St Luke, chapter 10, vs. 23].

But 'the Son of Man' is Jesus Christ's usual designation of Himself. In the *Old Testament* this title refers to God in the Book of *Ezekiel*, but in the Book of *Daniel* the title designates the Messiah, a being in human form. Jesus Christ, in referring to Himself as the Son of Man, usually does so in the context of suffering and of human sympathies: "The Son of man shall be delivered up to be crucified". [St Matthew, chapter 26, vs.2] Again, "For the Son of Man is come to seek and to save that which is lost". [St Luke, chapter 19, vs.10]. Jesus Christ's use of this title brings Him closer to the human nature which He had chosen to share.

It was an essential part of the process of redemption that He should fully experience our physical nature, especially with regard to physical suffering. On the day of His arrest before His Passion, Jesus Christ experienced the 'Agony in the Garden', knowing that His physical body was soon to be crucified, at which time He prayed to God the Father that, "if it be possible, let this chalice pass from me". But He immediately resolved, "Nevertheless, not as I will but as Thou wilt". [St Matthew's *Gospel* chapter 26, vs. 39].

The stages of the subsequent Passion, called the 'Sorrowful Mysteries' of the Rosary, are at the same time both real and representative of the sufferings experienced in human life. First, the prayer and agony in the garden indicates the agonizing moral choices facing humanity. Second, the scourging at the pillar indicates the physical sufferings of the human body. Third, the crowning with thorns symbolizes the mental sufferings of humanity. Fourth, the carrying of the cross represents the various burdens imposed on us in life. Fifth, the crucifixion and death of Our Lord represents our own terminal suffering and death. Jesus Christ, in being born in Time of a woman, is in the human sense the 'Son of Man', a fully human child, and therefore mortal. In order to die on the Cross He had to be born out of His mother's womb. In some respects His physical nature was a temporary limitation of His Divine Nature.

On Time and the Timeless

The physical body of Jesus Christ that was born to the Virgin Mary through the creative impulse of the Holy Spirit was sealed in the tomb after His death on the cross. In the early morning on the third day after the crucifixion, Mary Magdalene went to the tomb, only to find that it was empty. She ran to wake Peter and John who themselves rushed to the tomb followed by Mary Magdalene. They saw the linen cloths neatly folded, in which Jesus Christ had been wrapped. Then they returned home. Mary Magdalene, who had caught up with them at the tomb, briefly stood outside weeping; then she looked again into the tomb where she now saw two Angels sitting, one at the head and one at the feet where Jesus Christ had been placed. An Angel asked her why she was crying and she said simply that Jesus Christ had been taken away and she did not know where to.

At this point she turned back out of the tomb and saw a man who she took to be the gardener. The man asked her the same question of "Why are you weeping?" After asking the 'gardener' if he had taken Jesus Christ's body away, he says her name, "Mary", and at that point she recognizes Jesus Christ, her "Rabboni", or Master. He tells her of His imminent 'Ascension' to the Father, enjoins her not to touch His as yet 'un-ascended' body, but to announce His Resurrection to the other disciples.

She does so and on the same day Jesus Christ came to where the other disciples were gathered. He showed them the wounds of the crucifixion, the 'stigmata'. Then He breathed on them and said, "Receive ye the Holy Ghost", Who now gives them the spiritual authority to forgive or retain the sins of sinners. At this and at other times over the following days, the resurrected Jesus Christ shows Himself to His disciples, including to 'doubting' Thomas. According to St Matthew's *Gospel* the disciples were able to touch Jesus Christ's feet. St Luke's *Gospel* gives more detail: "See My hands and feet, that it is I myself. Handle and see; for a spirit hath not flesh and bones, as you see Me to have". [chapter 24, vs. 39].

Jesus Christ then eats fish and some honeycomb further to demonstrate his physical presence. But, it was His resurrected, transfigured body; not His body as it was at the crucifixion with His scourged back and His thorn-wounded head. Only the 'stigmata' were present in Jesus Christ's resurrected body - the five wounds in hands, feet and side. It is also a fact that when Mary Magdalene sees the figure of the 'gardener' by the tomb, she does not recognize Him as Jesus Christ. Only when He says her name does recognition come.

On Time and the Timeless

We do have, however, an earlier instance of the changed face of Jesus Christ at the Transfiguration. In St Luke's account we read: "And while He prayed the shape of His countenance was altered and His raiment became white and glittering". [St Luke's *Gospel,* chapter 9, vs. 29]. Confirmation of this comes from a similar occasion: the meeting with the men on the road to Emmaus which took place on the day of the Resurrection. Two followers, one of whom was Cleophas, were joined by Jesus Christ on the road from Jerusalem. He, as in the case of Mary Magdalene, was not recognized by them, and he held a long learned conversation with them: "He expounded to them in all the scriptures the things that were concerning Him". It was not until they arrived at Emmaus and were at table in their lodging that, on the breaking of bread, they finally recognized Jesus Christ:

> *And their eyes were opened; and they knew Him. And He vanished out of their sight.*
>
> [St Luke, chapter 24, vs. 31].

Again, it must be that Jesus Christ's resurrected face looked in some way different from what it was during the time of His crucifixion. There is no mention of wounds to His head, for example. Also, together with His physical presence on these occasions, He is able to break very physical bread, just as earlier He was able to eat fish and honeycomb. In His resurrected body, Jesus Christ has a very easy relationship with the material world and is able to assume its functions and to act within it. This should be no surprise: as one of the Three Persons of the Godhead He was able to create the physical cosmos and with the other two Persons, God the Father and God the Holy Spirit, He was able to intervene in the life of the physical world from time to time.

It is a reminder of William Blake's great insight: "Eternity is in love with the productions of Time". Indeed, it is not merely 'from time to time' that the Trinity acts in the cosmos: the Trinity is a permanent presence and active within it. In contemplating the end of the cosmos, Jesus Christ says, with authority, "Heaven and Earth shall pass; but my words shall not pass away." [St Matthew's *Gospel,* chapter 24, vs. 35; St Luke's *Gospel,* chapter 21, vs. 33].

This is in the context of talk about the Kingdom of God, and of the signs in the cosmos that will precede the Kingdom's establishment. Jesus Christ's "words shall not pass away" because they concern the spiritual, eternal realities of the Kingdom. It is a potent reminder to us that Eternity is the 'standard model' and the Earth, existing in time, is a 'special case'.

On Time and the Timeless

In talking of the resurrection of the dead, Jesus Christ is categorical in His rejoinder to His disciples:

> *And as concerning the dead that they rise again have you not read in the book of Moses, how in the bush God spoke to him, saying: I am the God of Abraham and the God of Isaac and the God of Jacob? He is not the God of the dead but of the living.*
>
> [St Mark's *Gospel*, chapter 12, vss. 26-27].

Jesus Christ's words are realized at the time of the Transfiguration when Peter, James and John see Him talking with the recognizable persons of Moses and Elias (Elijah), at the moment when God the Father's voice is heard in a bright cloud: "This is my beloved Son in whom I am well pleased". [St Matthew's *Gospel*, chapter 17, vs. 5]. At this moment we realize that the Kingdom of Heaven, the Timeless Mode, embraces all historical periods in the relationship between God the Father and His human children, not just those of the Christian period.

The prophets and patriarchs of the *Old Testament* have entered eternity already during Jesus Christ's lifetime on Earth; just as the saints and martyrs of the subsequent Christian period have done so. Jesus Christ's talk of the Day of Judgment at the end of the physical universe is the final act in an eschatology which concerns itself with the 'last things': death, judgement and humanity's state after death in the Timeless Mode. Interestingly, Jesus Christ gives no information about when the end of the physical cosmos will come. His answer suggests either that His Incarnation limits His access to Divine Wisdom, or that He considers it inappropriate for time-bound humanity to be able to anticipate the End of Time. He says categorically that "of that day and hour no one knoweth; no, not the angels of heaven, but the Father alone". [St Matthew's *Gospel*, chapter 24, vs. 36]. The "no one" ("no man" in other versions) would exclude Jesus Christ Who is "One" with the Father.

Cosmologists have calculated that our solar system is about 4.5 billion years old and that it will be another five to seven billion years into the future before Earth will be swallowed up by the Sun as it expands into a Red Giant. The solar system itself will cease to exist in one quadrillion (1,000,000,000,000,000) years into the future as the Sun itself cools after its White Dwarf phase. The terms of these events - both the astronomical numbers and the fairy-tale names - seem to us to belong to legend rather than to scientific fact! Partly because the timescale is of a totally different order of magnitude from the human life-span of 'three score years and ten'.

On Time and the Timeless

Even the time-frame of life on Earth, beginning with single-celled organisms, stretches back a mere four billion years; and in the case of ourselves, *Homo sapiens*, less than one million years (0.781 million years).

By these cosmological calculations we can be assured that the Earth has a long future ahead of it in terms of our 24-hour day or twelve-month year. These values for a day or a year compared with the time-values describing the future when the 'heat-death' of the whole cosmos is calculated to occur (10^{1000} years) are but as 'the blink of an eye'. It is fortunate for us that our human lives are concerned with days and years in all practical mundane matters.

Our brains simply find it difficult to comprehend astronomical, not to say cosmological, values of space and time. Even one light year (a measure of the distance that light can travel in one year moving at a speed of 186,000 miles per second) is extremely difficult, if not impossible, for us to conceive, except when it is expressed in purely mathematical terms.

It is almost as difficult for us as conceiving infinity and even more so of eternity, of Timelessness. We have the same mathematical symbol for infinity (∞) created by John Wallis in England in 1655, and for eternity (∞) designating, if you like, an infinite and eternal equivalent of the space-time continuum. The infinity symbol is not a mathematical quantity or process, because there is no way in which our human faculties can grasp the space-time continuum, and even less so the eternally infinite.

However, I suspect that the majority of people, even in our Age of Science, spend little or no time thinking about the nature and size of the universe in which we undoubtedly live. It may be that because of the daily reminders of death in all cultures we spend a little more time thinking about Eternity.

The various world religions focus our attention much more on the fate of individuals and their souls than they do on the physical parameters of the universe in which we live. Modern scientific measurements and models of the cosmos have in fact practically removed the religious or supernatural element from our current thinking about this universe. The fact of space travel and the landing of American astronauts on the Moon confirmed us in the view that the universe is a physical entity and that it is governed by firm physical laws (at least locally within our solar system). Before space flight began in the 1960s, even physicists and mathematicians were not sure that the laws of nature as we knew them on Earth would apply beyond its atmosphere.

There was a sigh of scientific relief when our telemetry worked in the vacuum of space and we were able to communicate with our space vehicles. In a sense, the secularising of the universe has freed theological discourse from some traditional but misleading religious concepts. Among these, of course, are the spatial implications of 'ascent' and 'descent' that I have discussed earlier in this book. These concepts did have some justification in models of the cosmos even after the Copernican revolution that displaced the Earth from the centre of the universe and set it in an elliptical orbit round the Sun. Before Nicolaus Copernicus (1473-1543), a Polish mathematician, the accepted model of the cosmos was that described by Ptolemy (c.100-170 AD), a Greek astronomer. Ptolemy's system placed the Earth at the centre of the universe, with the Moon, Mercury, Venus, the Sun, Mars, Jupiter and Saturn, in that order, in concentric circular orbits around the Earth. Beyond Saturn was the 'firmament of stars', an orbit including all the 'fixed stars' visible in the night sky. Each of the 'heavenly bodies' was embedded in a crystalline sphere, as was the firmament of stars. As these spheres rotated they produced (to us mortals inaudible) a musical chord, popularly called the 'music of the spheres' or heavenly music. Ptolemy's model effectively held sway for 1500 years. Indeed, when Copernicus published his heliocentric model, the Roman Catholic Church placed his book on the *Index Expurgatorius*, having concluded that his views, being un-Ptolemaic, were heretical. This action of the Church was taken in 1616, the year in which William Shakespeare died.

In his play *The Merchant of Venice* [Act V, sc. i, ll.60-65] Lorenzo explains this belief to Jessica:

There's not the smallest orb which thou behold'st
But in his motion like an angel sings,
Still quiring to the young-eyed cherubins;
Such harmony is in immortal souls;
But whilst this muddy vesture of decay
Doth grossly close it in, we cannot hear it.

It is clear from this that the Ptolemaic system developed over the centuries, and especially during the Christian Middle Ages, had a strong religious significance. Cosmology and theology here meet. This fact largely explains why any questioning of the cosmology, by Copernicus and by Galileo, for example, was seen as heresy. In the Ptolemaic model of the cosmos, beyond the sphere of fixed stars or 'firmament', was the *Primum Mobile*, the first mover.

This sphere of the first mover, being the nearest sphere to God, was kept in motion by God's love, and in turn transmitted this loving motion to the other crystalline spheres which held the other heavenly bodies. Thus the physical universe was sustained in its motions by the love of the Creator. Beyond the *Primum Mobile* was described by Aristotle as "neither place nor void nor time", which Medieval Christians believed to be the 'location' of Heaven and God. This cosmology can be found fully developed in Dante Alighieri's *Divine Comedy* [1308-21] and later in Geoffrey Chaucer's *Troilus and Criseyde* [mid-1380s]. This model of the cosmos clearly gave importance to place, to above and below. I remember very vividly attending a course of lectures on 'The Medieval Universe' given by C.S. Lewis at Cambridge in 1958-59. He began by asking us to imagine ourselves living within the medieval model of the universe. We live on Earth, which is the centre of that universe, and over our heads revolve the invisible crystalline spheres on which were carried the Moon, the Sun, the planets and the fixed stars. Beneath our feet, the centre of the Earth was a fiery region inhabited by Lucifer and his fellow Fallen Angels - Hell itself.

The knowledge that the heavenly bodies moved around us was in one sense reassuring, said Lewis, but it also meant that we were at the focal point of their influence, which was not necessarily benign. The 'science' of astrology was a consequence of that perceived influence. In addition, Hell was much closer to us than Heaven, and it was easier to 'fall' into it than to 'rise' through the seven spheres to Heaven. This, of course, is an excellent example of how spatial thinking has affected our moral and spiritual beliefs.

In clear contrast to this is our current model of the universe which puts us on the edge of the Milky Way galaxy amongst billions of galaxies and almost countless numbers of star-systems. The sheer extent, in space and in time, of this model defeats our normal comprehension. But, in another sense, it is liberating. C.S. Lewis described a very enclosed system, both physically and philosophically. Our modern scientific view has opened up the cosmos to our investigations and our imaginations, in a way that has encouraged a feeling of wonder at its enormous dimensions in space and in time. The numerical values for distances in space and for measurements of time on this scale are completely incompatible with our Earthly experience of these physical realities.

The Earth-centred, mankind-centred, model of Ptolemy, of Dante, of Chaucer and Shakespeare was much more comprehensible to Renaissance humanity than modern astrophysics is to us. The fact that our modern mathematics applies in the vacuum of space and on the surfaces of other heavenly bodies - the Moon, Mars, Venus, the moons of Jupiter - that our spacecraft have visited, was a great relief to America's NASA engineers in the 1960s. It has enabled us to escape the Earth's gravitational pull and to dispatch spacecraft to various destinations within our Solar System. But, in the context of the cosmos that the Hubble Telescope, for example, has revealed to us, it is like a sand-fly hopping from one grain of sand to the next! The main difference is that we, unlike the sand-fly, can measure the distance and the time taken to move between the two sand-grains. Nonetheless, in this vast cosmos we have not glimpsed Heaven nor have we found a metaphysical Hell!

Astronomy and cosmology **have** revealed to us a dynamic, expanding universe: in physical terms, a violent place where travel-speeds are almost unimaginable and where temperatures are beyond our comprehension. A universe in which Black Holes 'swallow' whole galaxies and in the process, if Stephen Hawking is right, create "a region of infinite density and the end of time". [*A Brief History of Time*, p. 94]. He does not go so far as to suggest that the way to a spiritual Heaven is through a Black Hole (!), but infinity and eternity certainly feature in his cosmic, not to say apocalyptic, scenario.

However, if we turn our telescope back to observe Earth we should be amazed at the very existence, not to say survival in this violent cosmos, of such a seemingly vulnerable blue ball. That there is life, of such amazing variety and complexity in every ecological niche, is truly astonishing; and that all the physical parameters of our solar system are 'fine-tuned' to support life is a source of wonder.

Charles Darwin, in the final paragraph of his book *On the Origin of Species*, 1859, writes:

> *There is grandeur in this view of life, with its several powers, having been originally breathed into a few forms or into one; and that, whilst this planet has gone cycling on, according to the fixed law of gravity, from so simple a beginning endless forms most beautiful and most wonderful have been, and are being, evolved.*

I am particularly struck by the metaphor that Charles Darwin uses to express the creation of organic life: "originally breathed into". He would know very well the religious connotation of this word "breathed" as it expresses the actions of the Holy Spirit in so many Biblical contexts.

On Time and the Timeless

The first is to be found in the Book of *Genesis*, chapter 2, vs.7:

> *And the Lord God formed man of the slime of the earth, and breathed into his face the breath of life; and man became a living soul.*

The Third Person of the Trinity, the Holy Spirit, the *Spiritus Sanctus*, means 'the Holy Breath' and the enduing with the Spirit is life-giving. In the above case of the creation of Adam, the Holy Spirit also initiates temporal existence, and is the sustainer of the cosmos.

Dr Erasmus Darwin, [1732-1801], (Charles Darwin's grandfather), in his epic poems *The Economy of Vegetation*, *The Loves of the Plants*, and *The Temple of Nature*, succeeded in giving a Deist's view of the cosmos and of the relationship between Time and the Timeless. He begins by acknowledging the agency of a loving Creator in bringing the cosmos into being, using an image that evokes the Holy Spirit:

> *When Love Divine, with brooding wings unfurl'd,*
> *Called from the rude abyss the living world.*
> [*Economy of Vegetation*, Canto 1, ll. 101-2]

But thereafter Natural Law was the Creator's method of maintaining the Universe in existence. The Deists denied whatever was miraculous in Jesus Christ's ministry, because empirical science needed an assumption that the cosmos, the natural world, was governed by the 'immutable' operation of physical laws that could be understood by human reason. So, Erasmus Darwin refers to God as the "Great First Cause" and the "Cause of Causes":

> *By firm, immutable, immortal laws*
> *Impress'd on Nature by the Great First Cause,*
> *Say, Muse, how rose from elemental strife*
> *Organic forms, and kindled into life.*
> [Opening lines of *The Temple of Nature*]

Erasmus Darwin in these poems begins to accommodate the Creation narrative to the findings of the New Science during the 18th century. Isaac Newton (1642-1726) in the previous century demonstrated the laws of motion that governed the material world. The 18th century, through the observations and calculations of astronomers such as the Herschel family - William, his sister Caroline and his son John who created a Star Catalogue - began to give us a larger vision of the cosmos, in both space and time.

This vision inspired Erasmus Darwin to see the natural world on the epic scale in his poem *The Economy of Vegetation*:

Flowers of the sky! Ye too to age must yield,
Frail as your silken sisters of the field!
Star after star from heaven's high arch shall rush,
Suns sink on suns, and systems systems crush;
Headlong, extinct, to one dark centre fall,
And Death and Night and Chaos mingle all!

The rhetoric here has a Biblical ring to it with echoes of the book of the *Apocalypse*: "and the sun became black as the sackcloth of hair...And the stars from heaven fell upon the earth." [chapter 6, vss. 12-13] Moreover, could that "one dark centre" be in modern parlance the cosmologist's 'Black Hole'?

The New Science emerged, of course, out of an older culture combining Classical and Biblical traditions, both of which are present as Erasmus Darwin imagines and articulates the Creation of the Cosmos in *The Temple of Nature*:

Immortal Love! Who, ere the morn of Time,
On wings outstretch'd, o'er Chaos hung sublime;
Warm'd into life the bursting egg of Night,
And gave young Nature to admiring Light!
You! Whose wide arms, in soft embraces furl'd
Round the vast frame connect the whirling world! [Canto 1.ll. 15-20]

It is an image of the Holy Spirit, before Time began, creating life out of chaos, 'hatching' the Cosmos and then lovingly sustaining it. "Ere the morn of Time" refers specifically to the Timeless Zone out of which the Holy Spirit emerges to initiate what we call the 'Big Bang' - here the "bursting egg of Night" - at which point or singularity' time and space are created. The "whirling world" of the young cosmos is calibrated lovingly by "Immortal Love". It is a relationship between the Timeless and Time in concord with the emotions of parental love, of storge.

The end of the world is, of course, a grand notion that has concerned people from the earliest times. It has taken on a special status in the current concerns about global warming and climate change. The end of civilization as we know it, if not the cosmic apocalypse, is being predicted by mainstream climatologists at the present time. James Lovelock, whose 1979 book *Gaia* expounded the idea that the Earth is a self-regulating life-support system, was interviewed in *New Scientist* in July 2019 and concluded the interview with this statement:

> *Perhaps I'm slightly religious, but I think the whole live part of the universe, which is mostly us and things* [on Earth], *is working through its existence. We'll just have to wait and see what happens.*

This is an apocalyptic vision and sobering from such a thinker.

Great changes and disruptions are likely in the way that humanity lives on planet Earth. We cannot know what the future holds for us as a species in the longer term. We shall, as we have done in the historical past, mould our environment to our physical needs in the interests of survival. Our increasing human population and the pressures this places on food production and on land and water availability will occupy us in all future ages.

It should be remembered, as the writer of the *Book of Wisdom* asserts [see p.1], that God's love embraces the whole of the cosmos, the whole of nature, not just humankind. In other words, the whole of the space-time continuum at every scale of existence is loved and sustained by the Trinity. This truth is expressed in the Creation account in the First Book of *Genesis*. At the end of each of the six days' work of creation, from the first light to the making of mankind, God "saw that it was good"; climaxing in verse 31: "And God saw all the things that He had made, and they were **very good**." [my emphasis]. The complete scenario is an expression of the pleasure and approval felt by the Creator for His Creation: the **whole** of it.

The Creation account in the First Book of *Genesis* and God's work of six days is the basis of the 'Creationist' ideology which promotes it as literal truth. This 'fundamentalist' ideology is in direct conflict with the empirical sciences and their materialist worldview. Erasmus's grandson Charles Darwin's Theory of Evolution, with its vastly longer time-scales and its secular principle of 'natural selection' as the source of all forms of life on Earth, has become the popular antagonist to Creationism. Both theories involve arguments around Time. If it is acknowledged that Evolution is a function of Time within the Space-Time Continuum, then as such it is in the same relation to the Timeless as Time itself.

On Time and the Timeless

The Deism of Erasmus Darwin in the 18th century postulated that an 'effect' such as the cosmos must have had a cause, and that all subsequent causes in space and time could trace their lineage back to the Great First Cause, a Deity in the Timeless Sphere.

Charles Darwin was brought up by his mother in the Unitarian Church, as were many 'natural philosophers', including the revolutionary chemist, Joseph Priestley. This Church rejected 'revealed religion' which included the Divine status of Jesus Christ, His miracles, and belief in the Trinitarian status of the Holy Spirit. Miracles were contrary to the concept of natural causes to which natural philosophers gave their allegiance. This particular apostasy was perhaps a necessary stage in the progress of empirical science.

Today, some scientists are more open to the possibility of a Great First Cause, especially in the fields of cosmology, biology, and genetics. The singularity of the Big Bang is now seen as an effect that requires a prior cause which, because the moment of the Big Bang was the beginning of Time, must be found in the Timeless Zone. Biology is now acknowledging that an event approximately 540 million years ago dubbed the Cambrian Explosion when fossils of new life forms appeared without precursors in the fossil record, a fact which puzzled Darwin himself, suggests an input of 'new information': another effect without a prior material cause. In genetics, the four-character digital code from which DNA is assembled and according to which it functions has no precedents in nature. This fact has become known as 'The DNA Enigma'.

These scientific questions have all arisen from our increasing understanding of the 13.8 billion years that have elapsed since the moment of the Big Bang. Fortunately our own individual lives are measured in decades rather than in eons. Nevertheless, our span of seven or eight decades is time enough to love others, to raise a family, and to contribute much to our human culture.

Consider what Leonardo da Vinci, Ludwig van Beethoven, William Shakespeare, Mother Teresa of Calcutta, Albert Einstein and Marie Curie (1867-1934) achieved in their various lifetimes. Marie, with her husband Pierre, separated out one tenth of a gram of radium salt from one ton of the uranium mineral pitchblende in 1902. Marie died aged 66 from exposure to radiation. Johann Sebastian Bach (1685-1750) had twenty children by two successive wives (his first wife died in childbirth) and in addition is considered to be perhaps the greatest musical composer and performer on the keyboard and baroque organ in the Western tradition. All this was achieved in a modest lifespan of sixty-five years. Mother, now Saint, Teresa of Calcutta (1910-1997) founded the Missionaries of Charity which is active in over one hundred countries and cares for many thousands of men and women dying from HIV/AIDS, leprosy and tuberculosis, as well as other charitable work with orphaned children.

Jesus Christ, the spiritual inspiration and role-model of many various saints, had but thirty- three years on Earth in which to complete his Divine work of spiritual teaching, of redemption for humanity, and of the revelation of God's completed saving work, fulfilling promises and prophesies made in the *Old Testament.* St Peter, Apostle, Pope and Martyr, had a little over thirty years after Jesus Christ's Crucifixion to establish the Church in Rome. St Paul had a similar number of years, after his conversion, to complete his missionary journeys before being beheaded by the Emperor Nero in Rome around A.D. 68.

The end for us comes with our own death, but we have an example and a promise - a covenant even - given to us by Jesus Christ. Time and the Timeless touch at the moment of our death - as the fingers of God the Father and of Adam anticipate a touch in Michelangelo's Sistine Chapel depiction of the creation of Adam. This same action of touching is an essential part of many of the miracles by Jesus Christ. In St Matthew's *Gospel* Jesus Christ heals a leper: "stretching forth His hand, touched him, saying: I will. Be thou made clean." [chapter 8, vs. 37] Again, in chapter 9, vs. 25, He brings the ruler Jairus's daughter back to life: "He went in and took her by the hand. And the maid arose." In chapter 20, verse 34, Jesus Christ restores sight to two blind men: "And Jesus, having compassion on them, touched their eyes; and immediately they saw and followed Him."

When Jesus Christ performed His healing and revivifying miracles, He was employing the powers of His Godhead. When we are transfigured at our death, all legacies of physical and mental disease and damage will be cancelled. Our transfigured selves will be perfect. The raising of Lazarus from death after four days in the tomb [St John's *Gospel*, chapter 11] is perhaps the clearest witness to the power of intervention by the Divinity in human physical reality. The restoration of sight to the blind, of speech to the dumb, of sanity to the insane, are all 'medical' miracles that heal the individual.

On Time and the Timeless

Other social miracles, such as changing water into wine at the marriage celebration in Cana of Galilee [St John's *Gospel*, chapter 2]; the feeding of the five thousand on five barley loaves and three small fish [St John's *Gospel*, chapter 6]; the miraculous catch of fish [St Luke's *Gospel*, chapter 5], are all illustrations of the ability of the Divine, the Timeless, to intervene in the working of the physical world on the small scale. They are also 'parental' acts of feeding. The quieting of the storm on the Sea of Galilee [St Luke's *Gospel*, chapter 8], and Jesus Christ walking on the water of that same Sea [St John's *Gospel*, chapter 6] are on the larger scale of action.

It is clear that while Jesus Christ shares our physical humanity He also has the ability to act, often in explicit company with the Holy Spirit, with Divine capacities. He can thus move in and out of the physical and the spiritual, of Time and the Timeless, at will. In so doing He is firm in reminding us that He does so in harmony with the loving will of God the Father. The effective interaction between the spiritual and the physical is nowhere more evident than in the miraculous conception of the Christ-child. St Matthew's *Gospel* is perfectly clear in his account:

> *Now the generation of Christ was in this wise. When His mother Mary was espoused to Joseph, before they came together, she was found with child, of the Holy Ghost.* [chapter 1, vs. 18].

The next occasion when the Holy Spirit accompanies Jesus Christ is at His baptism by John the Baptist. St John the Evangelist describes the event thus:

> *And John gave testimony, saying, 'I saw the Spirit coming down, as a dove from heaven; and he remained upon Him.'* [St John's *Gospel*, chapter 1, vs. 32].

St Luke has a very similar account: "And the Holy Ghost descended in a bodily shape, as a dove, upon Him." [St Luke's *Gospel*, chapter 3, vs. 22]. The voice of God the Father is also heard on this occasion. Another effective intervention by the Holy Spirit is among the Disciples at Pentecost:

> *And when the days of the Pentecost were accomplished they were all together in one place. And suddenly there came a sound from Heaven, as of a mighty wind coming; and it filled the whole house where they were sitting. And there appeared to them parted tongues, as it were of fire; and it sat upon every one of them.*
>
> [*Acts of the Apostles*, chapter 2, vss. 1-3].

On Time and the Timeless

Subsequent to this, the Apostles spoke in a way that was understood by listeners who spoke different languages. The Holy Spirit evidently has the power to overthrow the Tower of Babel [Book of *Genesis*, chapter 11], the building of which had brought about a plethora of human languages. This universal understanding points to the nature of language spoken and heard in Eternity. For community to exist in the Timeless Mode it must be the case that the transfigured souls either understand all human languages or that they share a common one.

At this point I should like to turn my attention away from the mainly spiritual, timeless aspects of existence to more material, though for us temporal creatures no less important, concerns. Modern astronomy with its powerful telescopes has presented us with a universe that is immense in space and time. It is also enormously dynamic in its physical processes, with Red Giants, White Dwarfs, Neutron Stars, Black Holes, Quasars, Pulsars, and Dark Matter among them. They might seem the characters and landscape of a modern epic. In addition, we have identified many, many other star systems, some of which support planets, or 'exoplanets' as they have been called, with accompanying 'moons'. Our own Solar System we now know is on the edge of the galaxy we call the Milky Way, and there are billions of these galaxies in the known universe. Moreover, the universe is expanding in every direction as we observe it, apparently with no set boundary. To visualize and realize our individual place in this immense physical reality ought to fill us with awe and wonder. Our modern conception of the universe is a far cry from the 'cosy' Ptolemaic model understood by our not-so-distant ancestors, and which made sense to them as an all-inclusive world-picture. Is it possible for us to make sense of the universe that astronomy and cosmology have revealed to us? Why is the universe so vast and so dynamic, for example? I believe that an answer is to be found in humanity's very existence on the Earth.

As I stated at the beginning of this book, the universe began 13.8 billion years ago in a super-dense 'point'. The 'inflation' or expansion of the universe continues to the present moment, and it creates time as well as space - the space-time continuum - as it expands. We measure that time in light-years, which is also a description of the time and space it has taken to produce inside stars the chemical elements - of hydrogen, carbon, oxygen, etc. - that are necessary for organic life-forms such as ourselves. We must believe that it could not have been done any quicker, given the laws that govern physical processes. It was the same for our Earth's organic evolution leading to ourselves, most of which took place eons before *Homo sapiens* opened its knowing eyes.

On Time and the Timeless

The Solar System and planet Earth could only be safe for life in a part of the universe that was stable for a particular period of time. That period of time, from the evolution of *Homo sapiens* to the present, is a unique consequence of the development of the universe. This period is also the unique concern of God, as Father, Son and Holy Spirit, since its apotheosis - the establishment of the spiritual Kingdom of Heaven - is to be its endpoint. It is the point at which the Timeless touches Time and transforms or transfigures it into ultimate Timelessness. This transfiguration of the Earth at the 'End of Time' is referred to theologically as the *Parousia*, the Greek for 'arrival' or 'presence', indicating the Second Coming of Jesus Christ promised in the *New Testament*.

Spiritual bodies will replace our physical bodies in exactly the same way that Jesus Christ was transfigured: not just at the event of that name but at His Resurrection and Ascension into Heaven.

Earth's natural history before the appearance of *Homo sapiens*, unfolding with the history of the cosmos, was necessary to prepare a biosphere that would be supportive of evolving life. This preparation involved countless forms of life, from blue-green algae to grass and trees; from single-celled marine organisms to the largest dinosaurs. It is instructive to consider that the evolutionary processes which led to humankind over so many eons of Earth's history were active quite unseen by any self-conscious creature. This history included mass extinctions such as that of the larger dinosaurs. Nevertheless, as a result of all the earlier upheavals - geological, geophysical and biological - we humans came to exist at a period of relative stability in the history of planet Earth. Furthermore, we have proved to be, in William Shakespeare's words "the paragon of animals", and to be at the top of Charles Darwin's evolutionary tree.

However, this fact does not elevate us above other creatures in all respects. A vulnerability to disease is a major problem for us, and not only is it a physical problem but an intellectual one as well. Charles Darwin lost his belief in a beneficent God and became an atheist when his beloved daughter Annie died in childhood. Similarly, the deaths of Marie Curie's mother when Marie was ten years old and of her older sister Zofia three years before their mother caused Marie to abandon Catholicism and become an agnostic. The issue was that if God was beneficent and omnipotent why did he allow such deaths? The death of a much-loved family member: a son or daughter, a mother or father, affects and wounds storge, parental and familial love. This is the deepest kind of love, whose source is the Trinity. It affects even if the bereaved has the consolation of religion and believes in life after death. I can confirm this from my own experience of the death of my first wife, Marie, mother of our daughter, Emma, from cancer in 2013.

The only justification I can offer, if I am with John Milton to "justify the ways of God to men", is a material one, and it is linked to the development of the cosmos. Stars, planets and their satellites, such as our Moon, are spherical. These are relatively stable bodies partly because of their shape, whereas comets and meteorites may be any transitory shape. The surfaces of spheres curve round to end where they began. This results in the Earth being a closed system, escape from which (as we know from the Apollo Space Program) is both technically difficult and takes a lot of energy. Thus we are in and of the natural world, the biosphere, and therefore subject to all the accidents and intrusions of animate and inanimate nature into our physical bodies. We may be killed by falling rocks or by a meningitis infection; we may be disabled by a car accident or by a genetic condition. We are connected with and dependent on (in every possible way) our Earth, the Solar System, the Milky Way galaxy and the cosmos at large. It has been said that at the atomic level we are made of stardust, but for the bacteria and other pathogens that colonize our bodies we are just another ecological niche. We become, after the death of our physical bodies, food for worms according to the economy of nature.

Therefore, during the lifespan of our physical existence everything that we do is natural: an expression of our participation in the events that characterize the life, and become the history, of the universe. But there is one characteristic that is special to us in the whole of nature: we have a dialogue with the Timeless, with God the Father, God the Son and God the Holy Spirit. Of course, the whole cosmos, the space-time continuum, has its origins and its sustenance in the Timeless, but ours is a special dialogue which, through the historical life, death and resurrection of Jesus Christ, has ensured that our souls in transfigured bodies can enter the Timeless after our physical death. We can be confident of this outcome, just as we can be confident that the ability of the Timeless to intervene in Time is an established fact. Jesus Christ reassured His Disciples: "And, behold, I am with you all days, even to the consummation of the world" (the end of time). [St Matthew's *Gospel*, chapter 28, vs. 20] These are Jesus Christ's words to the eleven Disciples after His Resurrection. Time was, of course, in the first instance conceived by the Timeless and was given the capacity to evolve into the life we know.

On Time and the Timeless

The complexity, variety and beauty of the physical universe, from the 'flowers of the field' to the 'flowers of the sky', are awesome to us. So are those other natural expressions of creative life: the canvases of Vincent van Gogh, whose night skyscapes are so explosive; the poetry of Fr Gerard Manley Hopkins ("Glory be to God for dappled things...He fathers-forth whose beauty is past change: Praise Him!"); or Sir Edward Elgar's oratorio, *The Dream of Gerontius*.

It is my hope - though I have absolutely no evidence for it! - that because "Eternity is in love with the productions of Time", the art, literature, music, science (even cosmology!) - all the natural efflorescences of human creativity - may find their way to the Timeless and be accessible to us in our transfigured bodies. The 'transfigures' of the artists and scientists will also be there, together with the communion of the Saints. We know from the *New Testament* that Moses and Elijah are there, so there will be many other familiar figures in the "many mansions" of God the Father's "House" [St John's *Gospel*, chapter 14, vs. 2], including members of our own family.

Death is a consequence of our Earth-bound, time-bound existence. It is a feature of the whole of nature and indeed of the entire cosmos. Just as planet Earth is moving in astronomical time from creation to destruction, so everything in the material universe is doing likewise. In the ecology of the natural world, life thrives on death - the survival of the predator at the expense of the life of the prey, followed by the death of the predator etc. etc. Thus all of matter is recycled, regenerated; and nature is so enormously prodigal as to make this a self-sustaining ecological cycle. Our human bodies are fully involved in this process as they exist in space and time.

However, our human bodies also nurture souls - timeless entities that grow in time but are not destined to die. They are the greatest justification of 'the ways of God to men': "out of this nettle, danger, we pluck this flower, safety" in the metaphorical language that Shakespeare puts into the mouth of Hotspur. If this were not the case, if humanity did not have this connection to the Timeless, to God, we should be living in a closed system whose only function was to recycle the material within it. Nothing, including humanity, would have any purpose or meaning outside of the ecological cycle: birth, reproduction, death. As it is, we can be eternally grateful (literally) that the Godhead, especially through the teaching and redemptive work of Jesus Christ, the Son of God, and of the Holy Spirit in collaboration with God the Father, has given us "the Way, the Truth, and the Life." It is a gift to humanity that reveals the possibilities of our spiritual nature and provides knowledge of what is offered to us in our time by the Timeless.

On Time and the Timeless

But then there is the issue of the Second Law of Thermodynamics, of entropy. According to this Law, matter can only change from an organised state to a disorganized one, from order to disorder. Entropy is an integral aspect of time, of the direction of 'the Arrow of Time', and it applies to all matter in the cosmos and indeed to the cosmos itself.

There is an argument, however, that the processes of growth of living organisms, even of life itself, reverse this Second Law. First, it is self-evident that what is temporal is by definition also temporary. But the evolution of the cosmos in general and of the living organisms on Earth in particular temporarily reverses entropy. It does so by using the Sun's energy to catalyse chemical and organic evolution.

The reversal on the cosmic scale that led to our Earth becoming generative and supportive of life has lasted for eons and involves much 'fine-tuning' of the structure and dynamics of the physical universe. It is a managed evolution, not one left to chance, because again as Albert Einstein said, "God does not play dice" with the cosmos. The reversal of entropy on our human scale is found not only in the life-cycle of our bodies but also by analogy in our intellectual and spiritual development over a time-span of decades.

However, the greatest reversal of entropy is to be found in the life and teaching of Jesus Christ. It is the promise of the Resurrection of our individual bodies after death, becoming in the process 'transfigures' - new bodies designed for a life-out-of-Time, and in themselves Timeless.

Dante Alighieri, in the final lines of his *Divine Comedy*, expresses the climactic experience of approaching God thus:

> *Eternal light, known to yourself alone,*
> *Knowing yourself alone, once, twice and thrice,*
> *In loving company yet on your own,*
> *The self-renewing well of Paradise Forever!*
> *All the circling thus unloosed*
> *Reflected light, which my eyes dwelt upon,*
> *And saw the way those swirling tints produced*
> *A painted likeness that my eyes fixed on*
> *Completely, for that likeness was of us.* [Clive James' translation]

On Time and the Timeless

Dante sees the Trinity first as three revolving coloured circles (the most perfect geometrical shape) that resolve themselves into the human face of God. Thus Dante's vision of God confirms that we are made in the image of God, that God is a Person, or, rather, Three Persons comprising the Godhead.

Dante's revelation is visual, but I believe that an equally, if not more, important aspect of the Divine is verbal. St John emphasises this at the opening of his *Gospel*: "In the beginning was the Word", and the Word is theologically identified as Jesus Christ. We may recall that Jesus Christ said, "Heaven and Earth shall pass ; but my words shall not pass". [St Matthew's *Gospel*, chapter 24, vs. 35]. The assurance here is that His teaching about the Kingdom of Heaven contains eternal truths.

God the Father's words are occasionally heard directly. In chapter one of the Book of *Genesis*, from a Christian perspective, two of the Three Persons of the Godhead are active at the Creation: God the Father and the "spirit of God". The Father expresses the Divine Will in words which are also instructions to the spirit of God who is active "over the waters", in verse two. The next instruction is "Be light made." The spirit acts, "And light was made", in verse three, while God the Father participates in the process: "And God made a firmament"* [verse seven]. In this way, words are the means for the Persons of the Godhead to communicate in the act of creation. It is also in this way that the Trinity is 'humanized' in the sense that 'relationship' is an essential part of being human. God the Father expresses this need in His creation of Eve as a companion for Adam.

The appearances in icons, paintings, and prints, of God, Jesus Christ, and of the Holy Spirit, are culturally determined. The Prophet Daniel is the Biblical source of the image of God as the 'Ancient of Days', a white-haired, white-bearded, white-robed figure as of an old man. The Holy Spirit as dove derives from St Luke's *Gospel* account of Christ's Baptism. [3. 22]

* "Firmament" here in the Book of *Genesis* refers to the whole of space between the Earth and the highest stars. We are told in verse eight that "God called the firmament Heaven"; in other words the "firmament" is the physical universe seen from the point of view of Earth. This fact feeds the confusion over the use of the word "heaven" in theological discussion. This is one reason why I prefer to refer to conventional "Heaven" as "the Timeless Mode".

On Time and the Timeless

At the baptism of Jesus Christ, God the Father speaks and the Holy Spirit in the form of a dove (the 'Paraclete') settles on Jesus Christ, the Son of God. The Son often speaks to the Father in prayer and especially strongly at times of crisis. In the Garden of Gethsemane we have the words of the Son's prayer: "My Father, if it be possible, let this chalice pass from me. Nevertheless, not as I will but as Thou wilt." [St Matthew's *Gospel*, chapter 26, vs. 39; St Mark's *Gospel*, chapter 14, vs. 36; St Luke's *Gospel*, chapter 22, vs. 42]. This is the moment in Jesus Christ's Passion known as the Agony in the Garden when He anticipates His crucifixion. Jesus Christ's words to His Father from the cross are also recorded in St Matthew's *Gospel*, chapter twenty seven: "*Eli, Eli, lamma sabacthani* " (My God, My God, why have you forsaken me?); and in St Luke's *Gospel*, chapter 23: "'Father, into Thy hands I commend my spirit.' And saying this He gave up the Ghost." The first words are those of an abandoned child; the second those of a trusting son.

I should especially like to emphasize that there is conversation between the Three Persons of the Godhead; that language plays a full part in the Timeless Mode of life. The gift of the Holy Spirit to the disciples at Pentecost - the gift of 'universal' language - comes directly from Eternity and is a foreshadowing of what we shall experience there. The Bible texts suggest that the Holy Spirit does not speak directly in His Own Person in Time but that He is more an active principle. The Holy Spirit spoke through the Prophets of the *Old Testament* giving them knowledge of forthcoming events, especially the events that would unfold in the life, death and resurrection of Jesus Christ.

The Prophet Isaiah (or 'Isaias', a name that signifies 'Jesus is the Lord') is most clearly informed by the Holy Spirit of events to come. For example, in the Book of *Isaiah* [chapter 7, vs.14] we read, "Behold, a virgin shall conceive and bear a son: and his name shall be called Emmanuel" (meaning 'God with us'). Perhaps the most memorable and beautiful employment of Old Testament prophecy, used to foretell the coming of Jesus Christ, is found in Charles Jenner's libretto for George Frederick Handel's oratorio *Messiah*. Handel himself said that he was never closer to Heaven than when he was composing this musical work. Perhaps this was Handel's way of saying that he was inspired by the Holy Spirit. Inspiration is one of the great active vehicles of the Holy Spirit and the outcome is always life-enhancing and beautiful. Dante sees the Three Persons of the Trinity as three intermingling circles of light. I see the Trinity as three family members in conversation: a Timeless conversation whose underlying motivation is love, indeed parental love, storge, and the desire to promote life, especially the life of the transfigured men, women and children after the time of their physical death. In this way the consummation of Time is to be found in the Timeless.

At the end of this Part 1, Emily Brontë's poem 'Last Lines', expresses wonderfully her vision of God; a vision perfectly consonant with my own:

LAST LINES

No coward soul is mine,

No trembler in the world's storm-troubled sphere;
I see Heaven's glories shine,
And faith shines equal, arming me from fear.

O God within my breast,
Almighty ever-present Deity!
Life—that in me has rest,
As I—undying life—have power in Thee!

Vain are the thousand creeds
That move men's hearts; unutterably vain;
Worthless as withered weeds,
Or idlest froth amid the boundless main,

To waken doubt in one
Holding so fast by Thine Infinity;
So surely anchored on
The steadfast rock of Immortality.

With wide-embracing love
Thy Spirit animates eternal years,
Pervades and broods above,
Changes, sustains, dissolves, creates, and rears.

On Time and the Timeless

Though Earth and man were gone,
And suns and universes ceased to be,
And Thou were left alone,
Every existence would exist in Thee.

There is not room for Death,
Nor atom that his might could render void;
Thou– Thou art Being and Breath,
And what Thou art may never be destroyed.

Emily Brontë (1818-1848)

Complementary *Meditations* of Thomas Traherne

Our Perception of Infinity [Third Century, No. 73]

If anything yet remaineth that is dreadful, or terrible, or doubtful, that seemeth to startle us, there is more behind that will more amaze us. For God is infinite in the expression of His Love, as we shall all find to our eternal comfort. Objects are so far from diminishing, that they magnify the faculties of the soul beholding them. A sand in your conception conformeth your soul, and reduceth it to the size and similitude of a sand. A tree apprehended is a tree in your mind; the whole hemisphere and the heavens magnify your soul to the wideness of the heavens; all the spaces above the heavens enlarge it wider to their own dimensions. And what is without limit maketh your conception illimited and endless. The infinity of God is infinitely profitable as well as great; as glorious as incomprehensible: so far from straitening [constraining] *that it magnifieth all things. And must be seen in you, or God will be absent. Nothing less than infinite is God, and as finite He cannot be enjoyed.*

The Contemplation of Eternity [First Century, No. 55]

The contemplation of Eternity maketh the Soul immortal. Whose glory it is, that it can see before and after its existence into endless spaces. Its Sight is its presence. And therefore is the presence of the understanding endless, because its sight is so. O what glorious creatures should we be could we be present in spirit with all Eternity! How wise, would we esteem this presence of the understanding to be more real than that of our bodies! When my Soul is in Eden with our first parents, I myself am there in a blessed manner. When I walk with Enoch and see his translation [lifting up to Heaven], *I am transported with him. The present age is too little to contain it. I can visit Noah in his ark, and swim upon the waters of the deluge. I can see Moses with his rod, and the children of Israel pressing through the sea. I can enter into Aaron's Tabernacle* and admire the mysteries of the holy place. I can travel over the land of Canaan, and see it overflowing with milk and honey; I can visit Solomon in his glory, and go into his temple, and view the sitting of his servants, and admire the magnificence and glory of his kingdom. No creature but one like unto the Holy Angels can see into all ages. Sure this power was not given in vain, but for some wonderful purpose; worthy of itself to enjoy and fathom. Would men consider what God hath done, they would be ravished in spirit with the glory of His doings. For Heaven and Earth are full of the majesty of His glory. And how happy would men be could they see and enjoy it! But above all these, our Saviour's cross is the throne of delights. That Centre of Eternity, that Tree of Life in the midst of the Paradise of God!*

* Aaron's Tabernacle. Aaron was the brother of Moses and the founder of the Jewish Priesthood. The Tabernacle was in Aaron's time a tent that was carried on the Israelites' journey through the wilderness to the promised land.

Complementary *Meditations* of Thomas Traherne

The Universe as a Work of Art [Fifth Century, No. 5]

Infinity of space is like a painter's table, prepared for the ground and field of those colours that are to be laid thereon. Look how great he intends the picture, so great doth he make the table. It would be an absurdity to leave it unfinished, or not to fill it. To leave any part of it naked and bare and void of beauty would render the whole ungrateful to the eye, and argue a defect of time or materials, or wit in the limner. As the table is infinite so are the pictures. God's Wisdom is the art, His Goodness the will, His Word the pencil, His Beauty and Powers the colours; His pictures are all His Works and Creatures. Infinitely more real and more glorious, as well as more great and manifold than the shadows of a landscape. But the Life of all is, they are the spectator's own. He is in them as in his territories, and in all these views his own possessions.

Infinity and Eternity [Fifth Century, No. 6]

One would think that besides infinite space there could be no more room for any treasure. Yet to show that God is infinitely infinite, there is infinite room besides, and perhaps a more wonderful region making this infinitely infinite. No man will believe besides the space from the centre of the earth to the utmost bound of the everlasting hills, there should be any more. Beyond those bounds perhaps there may, but besides all that space that is illimited and present before us, and absolutely endless every way, where can there be any room for more? This is the space that is at this moment only present before our eye, the only space that was, or that will be, from everlasting to everlasting. This moment exhibits infinite space, but there is a space also wherein all moments are infinitely exhibited, and the everlasting duration of infinite space is another region and room of joys. Wherein all ages appear together, all occurrences stand up at once, and the innumerable and endless myriads of years that were before the creation, and will be after the world is ended, are objected [presented to the view] *as a clear and stable object, whose several parts extended out at length, give an inward infinity to this moment, and compose an eternity that is seen by all comprehensors and enjoyers.*

Eternity Defined [Fifth Century, No. 7]

Eternity is a mysterious absence of times and ages: an endless length of ages always present, and forever perfect. For as there is an immovable space wherein all finite spaces are enclosed, and all motions carried on and performed; so is there an immovable duration, that contains and measures all moving durations. Without which first the last could not be; no more than finite places, and bodies moving, without infinite space. All ages being but successions correspondent to those parts of the Eternity wherein they abide, and filling no more of it, than ages can do. Whether they are commensurate with it or no, is difficult to determine. But the infinite immovable duration is Eternity, the place and duration of all things, even of infinite space itself: the cause and the end, the author and beautifier, the life and perfection of all.

Ourselves in Eternity [Fifth Century, No. 8]

Eternity magnifies our joys exceedingly, for whereas things in themselves began, and quickly end; before they came, were never in being; do service but for few moments; and after they are gone pass away and leave us for ever. Eternity retains the moments of their beginning and ending within itself; and from everlasting to everlasting those things were in their times and places before God, and in all their circumstances eternally will be, serving Him in those moments wherein they existed, to those intents and purposes for which they were created. The swiftest thought is present with Him eternally: the creation and the day of judgment. His first consultation, choice and determination, the result and end of all just now in full perfection, ever beginning, ever passing, ever ending: with all the intervals of space between things and things: as if those objects that arise many thousands of years one after the other were all together.

We also were ourselves before God eternally: and have the joy of seeing ourselves eternally beloved and eternally blessed, and infinitely enjoying all the parts of our blessedness; in all the durations of eternity appearing at once before ourselves, when perfectly consummate in the Kingdom of Light and Glory. The smallest thing by the influence of eternity, is made infinite and eternal. We pass through a standing continent or region of ages, that are already before us, glorious and perfect while we come to them. Like men in a ship we pass forward, the shores and marks seeming to go backward, though we move and they stand still. We are not with them in our progressive motion, but prevent [precede] *the swiftness of our course, and are present with them in our understanding. Like the sun we dart our rays before us, and occupy those spaces with light and contemplation which we move towards, but possess not with our bodies. And seeing all things in the light of Divine Knowledge, eternally serving God, rejoice unspeakably in that service and enjoy it all.*

*****

Eternity Revisited

Part Three: On Original Sin, and Storge (Parental Love)

Humanity lives with the conscious knowledge of the fact of physical death: a consciousness that is a step-change in the natural history of mammals. The story of Adam and Eve in the Book of *Genesis* has real relevance here; or should I say 'stories' because there are two different scenarios. In chapter one we have the first:

> *And God created man to his own image; to the*
> *Image of God he created him. Male and female*
> *he created them.* [vs. 27]

This act of creation on the "sixth day" is the culmination of the creation of the "beasts of the earth", making man in effect the "paragon of animals" in Shakespeare's phrase. Male and female (yet unnamed) will "multiply and fill the earth" [vs. 28]. Like all the "beasts of the earth" and "every fowl of the air", man will be vegetarian, eating seeds and fruit. This "Heaven" and "Earth" [vss. 8-10] bears little resemblance to the Earth as we mortals know it. The contradiction implicit in this Creation narrative, where God creates the universe in six days, stems from its temporal structure. This structure implies that God creates time concurrent with His creation of matter:

> *And God said: Let there be light made in the firmament of*
> *heaven, to divide the day and the night, and let them be for signs,*
> *and for seasons, and for days and years.* [*Genesis*, chapter 1, vs. 14]

And yet the inhabitants of this 'temporal' universe are to be immortal, timeless!

It appears that God has created a virtuous 'virtual' Paradise, with cumulative generations that do not experience death: in other words, procreation between male and female Immortals. The moral innocence of the beasts in the act of reproduction extends to include that of man and woman: "Increase and multiply." [vs. 28]

It is only in the second Creation story that death arrives, as a consequence of the now named Adam and Eve eating the fruit of the Tree of the Knowledge of Good and Evil. This Tree, a little off-centre in the Garden of Eden, could be called the Tree of Death, complementing the Tree of Life which was "in the midst of Paradise." [*Genesis*, chapter 2, vs. 9], that is, in the central position.

On Original Sin, and Storge

Eating the fruit of the Tree of the Knowledge of Good and Evil would, it seems, lift Adam and Eve out of the state of 'innocence' retained by other creatures, and bestow on them a moral sense which is derived from a knowledge and experience of mortality. This scenario suggests that God 'planted' the seed of death as a natural component of the universe, which would emerge as entropy and the Second Law of Thermodynamics. The second Creation story sees man formed "of the slime of the earth" [*Genesis*, chapter 2, vs. 7] and woman formed from a rib of Adam. Thus they are both of the earth, earthy, and they already possess a social dimension: "Wherefore a man shall leave father and mother and shall cleave to his wife". [vs. 24] They remain, however, as in the virtuous, virtual Paradise, "naked...and were not ashamed". [vs. 25]. They were still the "paragon of animals".

It was the warning to Adam concerning the fruit (usually an apple) of the Tree of the Knowledge of Good and Evil that "in whatsoever day thou shalt eat of it, thou shalt die the death" [vs. 17] that gave Adam knowledge of potential mortality. This knowledge separates Adam and Eve from all other creatures, a separation symbolized after the Fall by their covering of their organs of generation, a distinctively human practice. These organs are, in addition to being the generators of life, also the bestowers of death: "in my beginning is my end" [T.S. Eliot: *Four Quartets*, opening of the Second Quartet]. In this way the awareness of death defines the human condition in the temporal mode. These stories focus on the primal issue of the agency of Adam and Eve in bringing physical death into the world: "And, as in Adam all die, so also in Christ shall all be made alive." [St Paul's *First Epistle to the Corinthians*, chapter 15, vs. 2]. St Paul's diagnosis, joining as it does the beginning and the end of Christian eschatology, of the guilt of Adam and the expiation of the collective guilt of humanity by Jesus Christ, hinges on the judgment of God on Adam for his, and Eve's, disobedience.

The medieval theologian Peter Abelard (1079-1142) asked the profound question, "Could God not just have forgiven Adam and Eve?" in his *Commentary on St Paul's Epistle to the Romans*. It is a good question to which the answer should be 'yes' if Adam and Eve were actual people in an historical narrative. But they are not: they are simply characters in the theological script of an *Old Testament* morality play. Adam and Eve's Fall, their Disobedience to God: their eating of the fruit of the Tree of the Knowledge of Good and Evil constituting their 'Original Sin', and the consequent penalty of mortality on all subsequent generations of human beings, became standard Christian theology, mainly as a result of the views of St Paul and St Augustine of Hippo.

There is, however, a debatable flaw in their argument. If each new-born infant 'inherits' a state of 'sin', propagated down the generations by sexual intercourse (as St Augustine proposed), then at the moment of Baptism the child is granted 'remission of sins'. Churches of the East and West hold that baptism cleanses what in the Eastern Church is called 'Ancestral Sin' and in the Western Church, 'Original Sin'.

However, in some mysterious manner 'original sin' remains to be passed on to the next generation. The theological arguments around this important issue are unconvincing, simply because they are based on the hypothetical actions of the presumptive first Man and first Woman.

I can think of no better way to illustrate the problem than by quoting from John Donne's poem of 1601, *The Progress of the Soul:*

Man all at once was there by woman slain,
And one by one we're here slain o'er again
By them. The mother poisoned the well-head,
The daughters here corrupt us, rivulets,
No smallness 'scapes, no greatness breaks their nets,
She thrust us out, and by them we are led
Astray, from turning to whence we are fled. [ll.91-7]

This indictment of Eve and of all women, written just 400 years ago by a man who was to become the Dean of St Paul's Cathedral (1621-31) and a leading 'Metaphysical' poet, is a consequence of the Christian Church's teaching about the putative 'Fall'. Written later, in 1667, the poem that provides the longest narrative of the 'Fall', *Paradise Lost* by John Milton, has become a canonical text. It was the only non-scientific work that Charles Darwin carried on his *Beagle* voyage, for example.

Of Man's first disobedience, and the fruit
Of that forbidden Tree, whose taste
Brought death into the world and all our woe...

But the condemnation of Eve's daughters that we find in Book Ten of the poem is almost hysterically misogynistic and might be seen as a Miltonic aberration if it were not recurrent in our culture:

On Original Sin, and Storge

[Adam]: *Oh, why did God,*
Creator wise, that peopled highest Heaven
With spirits masculine, create at last
This novelty on Earth, this fair defect
Of Nature, and not fill the World at once
With men, as Angels, without feminine;
Or find some other way to generate
Mankind? [ll.888-895]

Milton's friend and colleague in Oliver Cromwell's Commonwealth Government, Andrew Marvell (1621-78), in his poem *The Garden* expressed a similar sentiment:

Such was that happy garden-state,
While Man there walk'd without a Mate:
After a Place so pure and sweet,
What other Help could yet be meet!
But 'twas beyond a Mortal's share
To wander solitary there:
Two Paradises 'twere in one
To live in Paradise alone. [stanza 8]

Making allowances for the literary trope, the 'Metaphysical Conceit', this poem indisputably trades on the indictment of Eve. Needless to say, Marvell never married! and these three seventeenth-century poets clearly demonstrate the adoption of the myth of Adam and Eve into arguments around sexual politics.

It is important to note that none of the *Gospel* accounts of Jesus Christ's teaching records Him using the phrase 'Original Sin', nor does He refer to Adam and Eve as the progenitors of human sin, just as He does not employ the concept of the 'Fall' in His teaching. The history of lapsarian theology begins with St Paul.

We do not now believe that the first humans were called Adam (this name being probably derived from the Hebrew word *Adamah*, meaning 'the dust of the earth' from which Adam was made); and Eve (her name in Hebrew is *Hawwah,* from *hayah* meaning 'to live', "because she was the mother of all the living." [*Genesis*, chapter 3, vs. 20]. The two names are clearly allegorical, just as the Garden of Eden itself is.

On Original Sin, and Storge

The Early Fathers' interpretations of the allegory of the Fall have bedevilled Christianity for the past 2,000 years: the doctrine that a moral entity, Original Sin, is transmitted to future generations through a physical activity, sexual intercourse. Linking sex and sin in this meta-causal relationship has created more problems for Christian culture than any other doctrine: not least the wholly inhumane, un-Biblical doctrine of a 'Limbo' for children 'outside' of Heaven where unbaptized babies were condemned to spend Eternity. No father, no parent, would conceivably so exclude their child from their proper home. Such a doctrine is in total conflict with the whole nature of parental love, of storge.

One year before the publication of *Paradise Lost*, in 1666 another garden and another apple entered Western culture. The garden was at Woolsthorpe Manor, Lincolnshire; a son of the house, Isaac Newton, was sitting under the tree when an apple fell to the ground. At the time Newton was a mathematics student at Cambridge University and the fall of the apple galvanized his thinking about a 'law of gravity'. His subsequent book, the *Principia Mathematica* (1687), is a seminal work in the genesis of the new empirical science. The paradigm shift in human history that made possible a change from a theological understanding of life on Earth to a scientific one proceeded gradually in the 17th and 18th centuries in Europe. The shift is celebrated in the work of Dr Erasmus Darwin (1731-1802) the grandfather of Charles, a major figure of the European Enlightenment. In his proto-evolutionary poem *The Temple of Nature* (1802) the Tree of the Knowledge of Good and Evil becomes an icon of humanity's pursuit of systematic scientific - that is empirical - knowledge:

> *Next where, emerging from its ancient roots,*
> *Its widening boughs the Tree of Knowledge shoots,*
> *Pluck'd with nice choice, before the Muse they placed*
> *The now no longer interdicted taste.*
> *Awhile they sit, from higher cares released,*
> *And, pleased, partake the intellectual feast.*
> *Of good and ill they speak, effect and cause,*
> *Celestial agencies and Nature's laws.* [Canto 2, ll. 439-446]

The actors in this scene are 'reconstructed Eves': young women taking part in a learned discussion with the Muse of History, Clio, and her Sister-Muse, Urania, the Muse of Astronomy.

On Original Sin, and Storge

Both Muses preside over the Natural Sciences. The "celestial agencies" refer to the laws of astronomy which, beginning with Newton's epoch-making work on the mathematics and physics of gravity, revealed a universe that could be understood by human reason. "Nature's laws" in many other fields of scientific investigation, focusing on cause and effect, began to be understood. In the Deist theology held by Erasmus Darwin, God becomes the Great First Cause one of whose Effects was the Earth and its creatures, as well as the wider cosmos. Adam and Eve were treated as symbolic characters.

From the mid-seventeenth century Botanic Gardens were planted all over Europe in an Enlightenment project to 'restore Eden'. In these gardens it was not Adam who named the plants but Carolus Linnaeus [Carl von Linné] with his binomial nomenclature - itself a triumph of reason. The twentieth century Eden Project in England, with its earth-made sculpture of Eve, is (playfully) explicit in its intention and is in a grand tradition of including our 'original parents' and indeed animals from the botanic garden's Biblical sourcebook.

There is a sense now that the Tree of Knowledge is no longer a risk but an invitation: to understand empirically the creation of the universe and to approach thereby a better understanding of God. The late mathematician and cosmologist Stephen Hawking held much the same position. He concluded his book *A Brief History of Time* (1988) with the following statement:

> *However, if we do discover a complete theory* [a mathematical model of the nature of physical reality] *it should in time be understandable in broad principle by everyone, not just a few scientists. Then we shall all, philosophers, scientists, and just ordinary people, be able to take part in the discussion of the question of why it is that we and the universe exist. If we find the answer to that, it would be the ultimate triumph of human reason - for then we would know the mind of God.*

Hawking's final phrase, "the mind of God", is more than a figure of speech or rhetorical flourish. I would put it in the same category as Albert Einstein's conviction that "God does not play dice" with the universe. Both ideas are consonant with the Deist belief in God as the Great First Cause, bringing into existence a universe governed by immutable laws of nature. If humanity's powers of reasoning - so the argument goes - are on a par with Divine Reason being derived from it, then it should be possible for us to understand the effective forces and the deep structures of physical reality.

This view is a legacy of the Enlightenment and its paramount belief in Reason. But if theoretical physicists did achieve a 'theory of everything', it would only describe in mathematical terms the materials, forces and functions of the temporal, material cosmos as we know it. By definition it would not tell us about the time-less, space-less mode of being that we call Eternity or Heaven. Neither would it tell us anything about the personal relationship between the Creator and His Creation. For this we must go to the life, death, resurrection and teachings of Jesus Christ, for their expression of storge, God's parental love for His creatures.

God, in the three persons of Father, Son and Holy Spirit, loves His children. Being made in His image we share His character. We receive and give parental love; we have an innate sense of justice; we exercise the spirit of mercy; we are intellectually brilliant; we have an understanding of pure and applied mathematics; we have a sense of beauty and show creative genius in literature, music and the visual arts; we love the natural world and celebrate it in our investigation and imitation of it; we love one another and exercise charity towards each other; we desire to alleviate the sufferings of others; we explore the many physical activities of which the human body is capable; we appreciate the inheritance of our culture from our antecedents, our progenitors in the human world. These are all capacities and virtues that we derive from the Creator, the Trinity.

However, the gift of free will - another Divine attribute - leads us into temptation, into succumbing to evil choices, which is why the Lord's Prayer asks the Father not to put us to the test ("Lead us not into temptation") and to "Deliver us from evil". The 'Fall' and the concept of 'Original Sin' dramatized in a temptation scenario in the Book of *Genesis*, comprise an allegory of the negative consequences of our freedom to choose. At the same time, this freedom is the prerequisite for love freely given.

Adam's 'Original Sin' is enshrined in the phrase 'the Old Adam', just as 'a daughter of Eve' may refer to a 'fallen woman' as in Christina Rossetti's poem of that title. The doctrine linked conjugal love with lust, rather than seeing it as the initiator and supporter of the family. We know from experience that conjugal love is greater in its expression than simple sexuality. It has emotional, moral, and spiritual dimensions that link it to the love of God for His creatures. To begin an account of human history with Paradise and consequently to describe humanity as degenerating, falling away morally from that imaginary starting point, is indefensible in terms of natural history.

On Original Sin, and Storge

Human development, as with that of other life-forms on Earth, is directed by certain categorical imperatives: sustenance, sexual reproduction and the security of the individual and of the family, together with issues concerning status, that we share with many other creatures. These basic necessities of life have been achieved by societies and individuals in varying degrees in different historical times.

The drivers of our choice of destructive uncharitable behaviour are evolutionary ones in the Darwinian sense: they have led to wild nature being described as "red in tooth and claw" by Lord Alfred Tennyson [*In Memoriam,* 1850]. They are imperatives that we share with all other forms of life; except that, in our case, we can choose **not** to be driven to damage others of our species in pursuit of them. The Ten Commandments are directed against what in nature are often survival strategies. Jesus Christ's injunction to 'turn the other cheek' and to 'love your enemies' is a radical challenge to evolutionary imperatives.

These imperatives direct the energies behind our mammalian nature as it lives and grows in time. But, in addition, *Homo sapiens,* from prehistoric times, has believed that there is a life after death in one form or another. There are many cultural expressions of this in ancient art and ritual practices. There was, however, no certainty of this, no demonstration in the natural and cultural history of humanity that this hope or belief was true. It was Jesus Christ's Resurrection in a transformed or transfigured body, followed by His Ascension, or transference into the Timeless Mode - all events testified to by His disciples and other followers - which demonstrated the fact of life after death. In the Divine plan there had to be some kind of paradigm shift from physical death available in the Timeless Mode.

This step-change was the purpose and the achievement of the life, teaching, death and resurrection of Jesus Christ. Thus, Jesus Christ, of human and divine nature combined, effected an historically verifiable, self-conscious development in the life of *Homo sapiens.* Physical death was no longer the end-point of human life but led to a transformed or transfigured existence in the Eternal or Timeless Mode. And this transfiguration is possible for us as individuals provided that we follow "the Way, the Truth, and the Life" which is Jesus Christ and His teaching. It is a Way that demands doing good to our fellow human beings, not evil; and that requires a love of God that will regulate our lives (I prefer the word 'regulate' to the word 'rule') in Time as well as in the Timeless Mode.

On Original Sin, and Storge

Seeing Jesus Christ's Resurrection, in its particularity, as a moment in humanity's historical development should not, I believe, be taken as time-specific nor exclusive to subsequent Christendom. It was a moment when the Timeless intersected Time and disarmed Time of its 'arrow'. So Jesus Christ's achievement should be seen as retrospective and universal in the Temporal Mode. The transfigured persons of Elijah and Moses were both seen with Jesus Christ at the moment of His Transfiguration: two *Old Testament* men whose physical bodies had been 'unavailable' for burial. Elijah had been taken up to Heaven: "a fiery chariot, and fiery horses parted them both asunder": and Elias [Elijah] "went by a whirlwind into Heaven." [Fourth (aka Second) Book of *Kings*, chapter 2, vs.11].

Moses died on Mount Nebo: "and no man hath known of his sepulchre until this present day." [*Deuteronomy*, chapter 34, vss. 5-6]. The only other man in the *Old Testament* said to be transfigured rather than physically dying is Enoch who "walked with God: and was seen no more because God took him." [*Genesis*, chapter 5, vs. 24].

In the *New Testament* it is only Mary, the mother of Jesus, according to tradition, who was 'assumed' into Heaven and has no recorded place of burial. It is clear that Mary, the daughter of Anne, a wealthy but childless lady of Bethlehem married to Joachim, was conceived following an intervention by the Trinity. This circumstance is the basis of her Immaculate Conception, rather than the doctrine of 'Original Sin'.

However, the key event in the time-bound historical development of humanity remains the Transfiguration of Jesus Christ, reinforced by His Resurrection from the dead and His return to the Apostles in His transfigured body on several occasions over a period of forty days. It has been suggested that these events constitute an evolutionary leap in the history of humanity. This, I believe, is to confuse two different modes of existence. Evolution is a material process, rooted and ramifying in space and time. But transfiguration is a threshold event in which a person steps from the spatial and temporal world to a mode outside of space and time. And this step-change has been happening throughout human history, whenever a person dies. If it were not so, the 'transfigures' of Moses and Elijah would not have been visibly present at the Transfiguration of Jesus Christ, Who Himself explains in talking of the Father: "For He is not the God of the dead, but of the living: for all live to Him." [The *Gospel* of St. Luke, chapter 20, vs.38].

On Original Sin, and Storge

That Jesus Christ's death on the cross is followed after three days by His Resurrection demonstrates the great change of modality that is life after death, which we shall experience in our transfigured bodies. Insofar as our transfigured bodies retain our identity, in some mysterious way, there is continuity between the change of modalities. There is, if not an 'evolutionary leap', at least a developmental process. Because God, since His creation of the cosmos, has been working inside space and time.

The prophetic books of the *Old Testament* themselves contain the particular developmental process which started very early in the history of the Hebrews: Moses, Elijah, the *Psalms* of David, Isaiah, Ezekiel, Daniel and others. In the Book of *Daniel* we find this prophecy:

> *And after sixty-two weeks Christ shall be slain; and the people that shall deny him shall not be his. And the people with their leader that shall come, shall destroy the city* [Jerusalem] *and the sanctuary: and the end thereof shall be waste, and after the end of the war the appointed desolation.* [Chapter 9, vs. 76]

Jesus Christ saw Himself as the culmination of this prophetic tradition; so that He could say to His disciples in talking of the end of time and the Last Judgment:

> *And this gospel of the kingdom shall be preached in the whole world for a testimony to all nations; and then shall the consummation come.*
>
> *When therefore you shall see the abomination of desolation which was spoken of by Daniel the prophet, standing in the holy place; he that readeth let him understand.*
> [St Matthew's *Gospel*, chapter 24, vss. 14 -15]

Even in the Classical Roman tradition, the poet Virgil [70 -19 BC] is held by the Roman Church to be a prophet, foretelling the coming of Jesus Christ in his 4th *Eclogue:*

> *Now is come the last age of Cumaean song: the great line of the centuries begins anew. Now the Virgin returns, the reign of Saturn returns; now a new generation descends from heaven on high. Only do you, pure Lucina* [the Roman goddess of childbirth, and of the moon] *smile on the birth of the child, under whom the iron brood shall at last cease and a golden race spring up throughout the world. Your own Apollo [the Sun] now is king!* [Verses 5-10. Trans. HR Fairclough]

On Original Sin, and Storge

Although the Christian prophetic interpretation of this Ancient Roman pastoral poem is open to dispute, I include it partly because the context of the Roman Empire is important with regard to the timing of the Nativity.

Jesus Christ was born in Bethlehem in a province of the Roman Empire during the imperial rule of Gaius Julius Caesar Octavianus. The new Emperor took the official title *Imperator Caesar Divi Filius Augustus* which translated literally is: 'Emperor Caesar Augustus, the Son of God'. He became Emperor in 27 BC and ruled over a wide empire with great skill, establishing what became known as the *Pax Romana*, 'The Roman Peace'.

It was in general the most settled period enjoyed by the various occupied peoples up to that date in Rome's 500-year history. The opening of the second chapter of St Luke's *Gospel* provides incidental testimony to the universal administration of Augustus's Empire:

> *And it came to pass that in those days there went out a decree from Caesar Augustus that the whole world should be enrolled* [listed in a Census]. [vs. 1]

The 'whole world' is, of course, the Roman Empire. At this time, the Virgin Mary was already pregnant with her son, Jesus. The subsequent thirty-three years of Jesus Christ's life coincided with a time in history when communications and travel extended throughout the entire Roman world under the *Pax Romana*. It was therefore the perfect time for ensuring that Jesus Christ's teaching could be spread by his Apostles and disciples by land and sea.

In evolutionary terms it might be compared to the timing of historical human development during the inter-glacial period of Earth's climatic history that we are still experiencing. Jesus Christ was born at the right time and in the right place. In fact, it could be said that the dimensions of time and space and the Timeless Mode intersected with geometrical precision. In terms of the Timeless Mode, also, the prophetic tradition which runs through the *Old Testament*, preparing the Hebrews for the coming Messiah, culminates in John the Baptist. He was conceived by his mother, St Elizabeth, in her old age: a conception described in the *New Testament* as miraculous. When she was six months pregnant, she was visited by her cousin, Mary, whose own pregnancy through the intervention in Time by the Timeless Holy Spirit began a few weeks later than Elizabeth's.

The timing of these preparatory events, the fact that John the Baptist was a relative of Jesus Christ, and John's later role as a "voice of one crying in the desert: 'Prepare ye the way of the Lord, make straight his paths'" [St Mark's *Gospel*, chapter 2, vs.3] reveals the orchestrating of events beyond the scope of any purely human agency. The climactic moment when Jesus Christ is baptized by John, and in effect begins His mission on Earth, is the clearest evidence of the Timeless intersecting with Time.

At this seminal moment (as recorded in the *Gospels* of St Matthew, chapter 3, vss. 16-17; St Mark, chapter 1, vss. 10-11; St Luke, chapter 3, vss. 21-22; and St John, chapter 1, vss. 32-34), the three Persons of the Trinity are active: God the Father whose voice is heard saying "This is my beloved Son"; the Holy Spirit manifest as a dove that settled on the Third Person of the Trinity, Jesus Christ. It is at this moment in history, when Jesus Christ was thirty years old, that the 'paradigm shift' in the timeline of human history begins.

Homo sapiens, whose wisdom is endorsed by Jesus Christ as reported by St Luke: "for the children of this world are wiser in their generation than the children of light" [the angels], in his *Gospel* [chapter 16, vs. 8], has come a long way in its development with regard to the things of this world.

The work of palaeontologists suggests that modern humans evolved some 300,000 years ago in Mesopotamia and Egypt, in India and China. These time-values are in the context of our current understanding of the age of the Earth as over 4,000,000,000 years. The progress of human knowledge may be illustrated with the dating by Archbishop Ussher in 1654 of the creation of the Earth as happening in the year 4004 BC. He derived this date by a learned study of the chronology of the *Old Testament* working back through the generations to the Creation story in the book of *Genesis*. The books of the *Old Testament* itself were written at various times between 1200BC and 165BC.

Our present wisdom concerning the scale and character of the cosmos, the geology of the Earth, the development of organic life including that of the various hominin species leading to ourselves, through both the fossil record and the unearthing of early artefacts, is indisputable, being the subjects of the science. In the case of artefacts, there is an astonishing increase in sophistication, in technical skill, between the earliest stone tools and the latest industrial robots, or between the possible use of the stone circle at Stonehenge as an astronomical instrument and a modern radio telescope. Indeed, when we consider the achievement of spaceflight, of *Homo sapiens* on the Moon, of the Hubble

Space Telescope launched into Earth-orbit in 1990, of our space vehicles exploring the planets and even the Sun itself, we might be tempted to think that this technological progress constituted an 'evolutionary leap'. However, it is our machines, not ourselves, that have developed. Compare this material advancement with the renewal of life after death: a transfigured life in a Timeless Mode of existence, and it becomes clear to us which is the most 'revolutionary' advance.

It should not surprize us that this existential leap, this 'saltation' as evolutionary biologists would describe it, should have been such a seemingly slow development in human history. On a scale of values that places the birth of the cosmos some 13.8 billion years ago - our Sun coalescing 4.6 billion years ago and the Earth a little less at 4.0 billion years ago - the 3,300 years since the prophet Moses received the Ten Commandments from God is but one tick of the historical clock. The life, death and resurrection of Jesus Christ 2,000 years ago is shorter on this scale than an intake of breath. In other words, it is a very recent development indeed in the history of the cosmos.

Nevertheless, it was the beginning of a process that will continue endowing humanity with the opportunity to imitate Jesus Christ in His faith in God the Father and in the exercise of storge, of parental and familial love for others. This opportunity is, of course, in the context of free will: the freedom to make choices with which the Trinity endowed Time's children. The story of Adam and Eve dramatizes this freedom, as we have seen. The angels also exercise their free will in the Timeless Mode, and some of them, traditionally associated with the angel Lucifer, chose not to accept the status of God as Father, nor to live in a loving relationship with the Trinity.

Jesus Christ in the *Gospels* is unequivocal about the consequences for individual souls of the wise or foolish exercise of choice: "You cannot serve God and mammon" (worldly interests). [St Matthew, chapter 6, vs. 24]. And again in St Matthew [chapter 7, vs. 13]: "Enter ye in at the narrow gate; for wide is the gate and broad is the way that leadeth to destruction; and many there are who go in thereat." Jesus Christ's fundamental statement that "I am the Way, and the Truth, and the Life. No man cometh to the Father but by me." [St John's *Gospel*, chapter 14, vs. 6] expresses the three aspects of His teaching. "The way" is defined by Jesus Christ's precepts concerning our relationship to God the Father, and to our fellow human beings: storge, the love between parent and child. "The truth" is the eternal unity between Jesus Christ Himself and

On Original Sin, and Storge

God the Father: "Philip, he that seeth me seeth the Father also." [St John's *Gospel*, chapter 14, vs. 9]. "The Life" is the timeless life-after-death that Jesus Christ's Resurrection has made available to all humanity.

The corollary to this is, of course, that if we do not choose "the Way", and do not accept "the Truth", then "the Life" may not be available to us in its Timeless Mode: "If any abide not in Me he shall be cast forth as a branch and shall wither; and they shall gather him up and cast him into the fire; and he burneth." [St John's *Gospel*, chapter 15, vs. 6].

The Parable of the Talents in St Matthew's *Gospel* carries the same message: "For to everyone that hath shall be given, and he shall abound: but, from him that hath not, that also which he seemeth to have shall be taken away." [chapter 25, vs. 29].

Jesus Christ is always unequivocal about the consequences of our choices of word and action during our earthly lives. Options arise from our possession of free will, and our freedom to act either out of charity, which I identify with storge, or out of enmity towards other people.

In choosing between the opposites of love and hate the experience we enjoy of our own parents' love for us encourages us to choose love. Historically, the experience that the twelve disciples and others had of Jesus Christ's love for them - experienced through so many instances of caring, compassion and healing - consolidated their own life-changing response to Jesus Christ.

God is Love, as we know to be a fact from Jesus Christ's life and teaching. The Father's love for His own 'beloved Son', for His angels, and for us as His children on Earth, is what I have called storge, parental love. Another Greek word *Agape*, denoting 'spiritual love', is traditionally and currently used to express the loving relationship between the Trinity and humanity. The Latin word *caritas*, translated as 'charity', is also used in this context, especially in the *Epistles* of St Paul: "And hope confoundeth not; because the charity of God is poured forth in our hearts, by the Holy Ghost who is given to us." [*To the Romans*, chapter 5, vs. 5]; and "Loving one another with the charity of brotherhood." [chapter 12, vs. 10].

Charity is one of the three theological virtues: faith, hope and charity, and its usual dictionary definition is 'universal love'. However, the word is currently used to denote almsgiving to those in need of help. It is because of the impersonal connotations of

'Agape' and of 'Charity' in modern discourse that I prefer the word storge, parental love, since I believe it describes most accurately the emotional bond between the Trinity and us as children of God. It is the kind of love that impels parents to endanger, **even to sacrifice,** their own life, to save their child.

In the light of Jesus Christ's statement that "I and the Father are One" [St John's *Gospel*, chapter 10, vs. 30], His relationship - and that of the Holy Spirit - to humanity is that of Father. His love for us, expressed most powerfully through His self-sacrifice, is therefore storge. Exactly this relationship is articulated in His lament over Jerusalem: "How often would I have gathered together thy children, as the hen doth gather her chickens under her wings, and thou wouldest not?" [St Matthew's *Gospel*, chapter 23, vs. 37; St Luke's *Gospel*, chapter 13, vs. 34].

Storge, as we see in Jesus Christ's choice of image, is not confined to humanity but is shared by all God's creatures. Konrad Lorenz, the 20th century zoologist who studied the behaviour of birds in their natural habitat, concluded that a process he called 'imprinting' was crucial to the successful rearing of hatchlings. The body of the parent bird imprints itself on the senses of the offspring. The same is true of ourselves: without the touch, smell, and taste of a loving mother very shortly after birth, a child may not thrive.

Parental love is absolutely at the heart of God's creation and of His creatures. The bond between parents and their offspring is an expression of divine love. It is notable that in Jesus Christ's lament over Jerusalem the image he chooses is that of a hen with her chickens: a maternal example of storge. It should suggest to us that the Father, Son and Holy Spirit are both paternal and maternal in Their love for Their children. This is the emotional context in which Jesus Christ conducts His ministry: "And Jesus, calling unto Him a little child, set him in the midst of them, / And said: 'I say to you, unless you become converted and become as little children, you shall not enter into the kingdom of heaven." [St Matthew's *Gospel*, chapter 18, vss. 2-3]. The quality of childhood that Jesus Christ refers to here - since it is not childish innocence, which is irretrievably lost in the adult - is the absolute trust that the child has in the parent. This kind of trust is what we need to cultivate as adults in our approach to the Trinity, whose children we all are. Jesus Christ's parable of the Prodigal Son is a wonderful expression of the father's enduring love for his errant son. [St Luke's *Gospel*, chapter 15, vss. 11-32].

But perhaps the most wonderful instances of storge are to be found in the events of Christmas and Easter. At the heart of Christmas is the birth of Jesus, the Son of God, to the Virgin Mary. At this moment God experiences the love of His Mother. God, in the Person of Jesus, also benefits from the protective care of His stepfather, Joseph. His mother, Mary, is a presence throughout His life: from the first miracle (changing water to wine at her request at the wedding in Cana) to His Crucifixion, when Jesus commends her to the family care of John:

> *Now there stood by the cross of Jesus, His mother and His Mother's sister, Mary of Cleophas, and Mary Magdalene. When Jesus therefore had seen His mother and the disciple standing, whom He loved* [John himself], *He saith to His mother: Woman behold thy son. After that, He saith to the disciple: Behold thy mother. And from that hour the disciple took her to his own.* [St John's *Gospel*, chapter 19, vss. 25-7].

So Jesus' final words to His mother restore her to a parental relationship for the remainder of her life. It is a restoration of storge. This is not, however, God's final gesture with regard to His earthly mother. In an act of filial love He transfigures His mother's body at her death and 'assumes' it into the Timeless Mode. Consequently, the Mother of God's body does not become 'dust to dust' and she has no known burial place in consequence. This act of love, according to psychologist Carl Jung, establishes a feminine presence with the Trinity.

However great, and theologically and historically important, the rôle of the Virgin Mary, the Mother of God, is, her pre-eminence as the feminine complement to a 'male' Trinity may have deflected the church from considering a 'female' identity in any one of the Three Persons. I like to think of the Holy Spirit as *Sancta Sophia* (Holy Wisdom) with the name's feminine gender in Latin. Jesus Christ's promise before His return to the Timeless Mode [St John's *Gospel*, chapter 14, vs. 16], expresses a mother's love: "I will not leave you orphans." [vs. 18]. It is the same as the joining of His mother, Mary, and John at the crucifixion so that she will not be left childless.

The feminine gender must arise as a creative impulse from the heart of the Trinity: like the male (Adam) the female (Eve) is made in the image of God. Michelangelo's fresco of the creation of Adam depicts God the Father protecting with His left arm the person of Eve, who is there in the Timeless Zone ready to join Adam in Paradise. We too should place the feminine at every level in the life of the Church.

*****

On Original Sin, and Storge

The medieval mystic, Dame Julian of Norwich [1342-1413], expresses the nature of storge in relation to God most explicitly in her *Revelations of Divine Love* [1373]. In chapter 60 she writes:

This fair lovely word Mother, it is so sweet and so kind itself that it may not verily be said of none but him; and to her that is very mother of him and of all. To the property of Motherhood belongeth kind love, wisdom, and knowledge; and it is good; for though it be so that our bodily forthbringing be but little, low, and simple in regard of our ghostly forthbringing, yet it is he that doeth it in the creatures by whom that it is done. The kind, loving Mother that witteth and knoweth the need of her child, she keepeth it full tenderly, as the kind and condition of Motherhood will. And as it waxeth in age, she changeth her working, but not her love. And when it is waxen of more age, she suffereth that it be beaten in breaking down of vices, to make the child receive virtues and graces. This working, with all that be fair and good, our Lord doeth it in them by whom it is done: thus he is our Mother in kind by the working of grace in the lower part for love of the higher part. And he willeth that we know this: for he will have all our love fastened to him. And in this I saw that all our duty that we owe, by God's bidding, to Fatherhood and Motherhood, for reason of God's Fatherhood and Motherhood is fulfilled in true loving of God; which blessed love Christ worketh in us. And this was shewed in all [the "Revelations"] *and especially in the high plenteous words where he saith: 'It is I that thou lovest.'*

This is a passage of great insight that goes to the heart of Christianity, and one that we in the 21st century need to recover.

*****

Complementary *Meditations* of Thomas Traherne

Questioning Original Sin [Third Century, No.8]

Had any man spoken of it, it had been the most easy thing in the world, to have taught me, and to have made me believe that Heaven and Earth was God's House, and that He gave it me. That the Sun was mine, and that men were mine, and that cities and kingdoms were mine also: that earth was better than gold, and that water, every drop of it was a precious jewel. And that these were great and living treasures: and that all riches whatsoever else was dross in comparison. From whence I clearly find how docile our Nature is in natural things, were it rightly entreated. And that our misery proceedeth ten thousand times more from the outward bondage of opinion and custom, than from any inward corruption or depravation of Nature: and that it is not our parents' loins, so much as our parents' lives, that enthrals and blinds us. Yet is all our corruption derived from Adam: inasmuch as all the evil examples and inclinations of the world arise from his sin. But I speak it in the presence of God and of Our Lord Jesus Christ, in my pure primitive virgin light, while my apprehensions were natural and unmixed, I cannot remember but that I was ten thousand times more prone to good and excellent things than evil. But I was quickly tainted and fell by others.

Storge [First Century, No. 52]

Love has a marvellous property of feeling in another. It can enjoy in another, as well as enjoy Him. Love is an infinite treasure to its object, and its object is so to it. God is Love, and you are His object. You are created to be His Love; and He is yours. He is happy in you when you are happy: as parents in their children. He is afflicted in all your afflictions. And whosoever toucheth you, toucheth the apple of His eye. Will you not be happy in all His enjoyments? He feeleth in you; will not you feel in Him? He hath obliged you to love Him. And if you love Him, you must of necessity be Heir of the World, for you are happy in Him. All His praises are your joys, all His enjoyments are infinite and eternal space: And like a gentleman's house to one that is travelling, it is a long time before you come into it, you pass it in an instant, and leave it forever. The Omnipresence and Eternity of God are your fellows and companions. And all that is in them ought to be made your familiar treasure. Your understanding comprehends the World like the dust of a balance, measures Heaven with a span, and esteems a thousand years but as one day. So that Great, Endless, Eternal Delights are only fit to be its enjoyments.

Complementary *Meditations* of Thomas Traherne

Jesus Christ Dies for His Children [Fourth Century, No. 56]

"No man loves, but he loves another more than himself." In mean instances this is apparent. If you came into an orchard with a person you love, and there be but one ripe cherry, you prefer [prioritize] *it to the other. If two lovers delight in the same piece of meat, either takes pleasure, and more esteems the beloved's satisfaction. What ails men that they do not see it? In greater cases this is evident. A mother runs upon a sword to save her beloved. A father leaps into the fire to fetch out his beloved. Love brought Christ from Heaven to die for His beloved. It is in the nature of love to despise itself, and to think only of its beloved's welfare. Look to it; it is not right love that is otherwise. Moses and St Paul were no fools. God make me one of their number. I am sure nothing is more acceptable to Him, than to love others so as to be willing to imperil even one's own soul for their benefit and welfare.*

On Becoming a Little Child [Third Century, No. 5]

Our Saviour's meaning when He said, "He must be born again and become a little child that will enter into the Kingdom of Heaven" is deeper far than is generally believed. It is not only on a careless reliance upon Divine Providence, that we are to become little children, or in the feebleness and shortness of our anger and simplicity of our passions, but in the peace and purity of all our soul. Which purity also is a deeper thing than is commonly apprehended. For we must disrobe ourselves of all false colours and unclothe our souls of evil habits; all our thoughts must be infant-like and clear: the powers of our soul free from the leaven of this world and disentangled from men's deceits and customs. Grit in the eye or yellow jaundice will not let a man see those objects truly that are before it. And therefore it is requisite that we should be as very strangers to the thoughts, customs, and opinions of men in this world, as if we were but little children. So those things would appear to us only which do to children when they are first born. Ambitions, trades, luxuries, inordinate affections, casual and accidental riches invented since the fall, would be gone, and only those things appear, which did to Adam in Paradise, in the same light and in the same colours: God in His works, Glory in the light, Love in our parents, men, ourselves, and the face of Heaven: every man naturally seeing those things, to the enjoyment of which he is naturally born.

THE COLLAR by George Herbert [1593-1633]

I struck the board, and cry'd. 'No more;
I will abroad.'
What, shall I ever sigh and pine?
My lines and life are free; free as the road,
Loose as the winde, as large as store.
Shall I be still in suit?
Have I no harvest but a thorn
To let me bloud, and not restore
What I have lost with cordial fruit?
Sure there was wine
Before my sighs did drie it; there was corn
Before my tears did drown it;
Is the yeare only lost to me?
Have I no bayes to crown it,
No flowers, no garlands gay? All blasted?
All wasted?
Not so, my heart; but there is fruit,
And thou hast hands.
Recover all thy sigh-blown age
On double pleasures; leave thy cold dispute
Of what is fit and not; forsake thy cage,
Thy rope of sands
Which petty thoughts have made; and make to thee
Good cable, to enforce and draw,
And be thy law,
While thou didst wink and wouldst not see.
Away! Take heed;
I will abroad.
Call in thy death's-head there, tie up thy fears;
He that forebears
To suit and serve his need
Deserves his load.
But as I rav'd and grew more fierce and wilde
At every word,
Methought I heard one calling, 'Childe';
And I reply'd, 'My Lord.'

Epilogue

Our life in Time is only part of a greater story that merges with the Timeless. In my Author's Note at the beginning of this essay I described how, after the death of my late wife, Marie, I shouted into the night sky, 'Where are you?'. It was a question that erupted instinctively from the heart of storge, even though I knew that her soul had gone home to the Trinity.

In 1988 while Marie was undergoing major surgery for cancer, she had a vision of Jesus Christ Who said to her that she had a choice: to come immediately to Him or to return to her earthly life. As He spoke, she looked down at the Earth and saw me, a solitary figure with spade in hand, laboriously digging. She felt for my loneliness and told Jesus Christ that she chose to return to me; which, with the help of Dr Pritam Singh's skilful healing hands, she did. Mercifully she lived another twenty-five years, long enough to support our daughter, Emma, in bringing up our three grandsons: Peter, William, and Nicholas. To Emma I am particularly grateful for her strong family feeling, and for the beautiful and reassuring images of the natural world that her professional photography and her literary talents have continued to capture over time. They have been a particular reminder of the Divine Treasure that is the natural world during the recent pandemic.

Marie was a well-spring of storge to her wider family. But, in particular she insisted, in the late stages of her terminal cancer, that I should re-marry after her death, aged 66. After a period of time, I married Philomena, a widow and retired nurse, from our church congregation. From Philomena's well-established and practised religious life I have learnt to be more devotional in my everyday living. It is in no small measure due to Philomena that I have come to write this book in the form that it is. I thank God for His Grace in bringing us together in such timely fashion.

The aim of this book has been in large part to make God, the Three Persons of the Trinity, more familiar, or perhaps familial, to us. All too often we approach God only through institutions. However important that is and has been in historical time in keeping the memory of God alive in our culture, I believe it is equally important to **domesticate** the Divinity. For this purpose we may need to revise our image of God - Father, Son, and Holy Spirit - and re-emphasise the parental relationship that the Trinity has with us; a relationship in which storge is the fundamental emotion.

Finally, this Meditation has provided, in the most unequivocal manner, the answer to my original question after Marie's death: "Where are You?"

The Authors

Main Text

Stuart Harris, MA (Cantab.), MPhil. (Sheffield), PGCE (London), was born in 1939. English literature teacher, Erasmus Darwin scholar, author, editor and independent publisher, church organist.

*****

Complementary Text

Thomas Traherne, MA (Oxon.), BD (Oxon.), was born in 1637. Ordained Priest in the Church of England in 1660, Rector of Credenhill, Herefordshire. Theologian, poet, and religious writer. He died in 1674.

*****